Do This,
Remembering Me

The Spiritual Care of Those
with Alzheimer's and Dementia

COLETTE BACHAND-WOOD

Morehouse Publishing
NEW YORK

Unless otherwise noted, the Scripture quotations contained herein are from the New Revised Standard Version Bible, copyright © 1989 by the Division of Christian Education of the National Council of Churches of Christ in the U.S.A. Used by permission. All rights reserved.

Morehouse Publishing, 19 East 34th Street, New York, NY 10016

Morehouse Publishing is an imprint of Church Publishing Incorporated.

www.churchpublishing.org

Cover design by Laurie Klein Westhafer
Typeset by Denise Hoff

Library of Congress Cataloging-in-Publication Data
Names: Bachand-Wood, Colette.
   Title: Do this, remembering me : the spiritual care of those with
   Alzheimer's and dementia / Colette Bachand-Wood.
Description: New York : Morehouse Publishing, 2016. |
   Includes bibliographical references.
Identifiers: LCCN 2015035479| ISBN 978-0-8192-3251-9 (pbk.) |
   ISBN 978-0-8192-3252-6 (ebook)
Subjects: LCSH: Alzheimer's disease—Patients—Religious life. |
Dementia—Patients—Religious life. | Alzheimer's disease—Patients—
Care. | Dementia—Patients—Care. | Caring—Religious aspects—
Christianity | Alzheimer's disease—Religious aspects—Christianity. |
Dementia—Religious aspects—Christianity.
Classification: LCC BV4910.6.A55 B33 2016 | DDC 259/.4196831—dc23
LC record available at http://lccn.loc.gov/2015035479

Printed in the United States of America

To all of the brave people who live with Alzheimer's and dementia, and those who love them.

Contents

————••—•—

Acknowledgments

———•◆•———

There have been so many teachers along the way including the many, many people living with Alzheimer's and dementia who have let me into their lives as spiritual caregiver. They are blessed teachers who spoke in many cases not with words, but always with their spirit.

It was the early patients I had in hospice as a chaplain who got this book started. Friend, teacher, and wise sage Joan Wright, who is a geriatric care manager, opened the world of Alzheimer's to me, not only with stories of her own journey with her mother, but by her coaching when we worked together at a local VNA and hospice agency. She encouraged me to go out and begin this research, she listened, gave advice, and I am very grateful. There were several nursing homes and adult day care facilities in southeastern Massachusetts that let me into their world to try out some of my ideas and learn. Thank you to friend Richard Johnson who died of cancer just as this book went to production, but who helped open doors in the senior living community. To Teepa Snow from Positive Approach who shared her wisdom with me, and to all the other professionals who agreed to be interviewed for this book, a heartfelt thank you.

Thank you to my dear friend Kim Harriman who was so encouraging and shared the excitement of getting published each step of the way; and to Kate Granigan, longtime soul sister whose love for the geriatric community is shared and whose work as a geriatric care manager inspires me daily. Thank you to my parish of All Saints Episcopal Church in Whitman, Massachusetts that has given me the honor of serving as their rector. Thank you to Sharon Pearson whose editing skills helped me believe all things were possible.

And to my family, husband Russ and the two beautiful young women we call our daughters, Adrienne and Bridget: there can never be enough words to say how grateful I am for you and how deeply you are loved.

And finally to my parents: to Mom, Barbara, who was an unbelievable, tireless, and courageous care partner to Dad in his dementia years and who is always my cheerleader; and to Richard, my dad, my Huckleberry Friend, and hero.

Foreword

———◆◆◆———

Over the years, I have had many names for my husband. Mostly I call him Q, of course, but sometimes I use his given name, Richard. I have called him by his childhood nickname, Edge, which comes from his middle name, Edgecombe. But I have also called him Honey and Honey Man and Sweetheart and Sweetie and Love and Handsome. Sometimes I have called him Dr. Quaintance or Professor. Sometimes I have called him Sir.

I have never called him *Baby*. In all these years, never.

Suddenly, though, I sometimes hear myself doing it. Sometimes, I call him *Baby*.

No, Baby, we're fine, I say when he worries that I've made a wrong turn driving. *This is the way. You'll see.*

Look, Baby, over there. See? To the right. Over to the right. The RIGHT—look where I'm pointing. Over there.

I do not decide to do this. Truth is, I've never loved hearing couples call each other *Baby*, though it's certainly none of my business what lovers call each other. But *Baby* as a term of endearment had just never been part of the dialect we use only with each other. Every couple has its own dialect, and *Baby* has never figured in ours.

Every time I address him this way, I shock myself. *Where did THAT come from?* Why *Baby*, after all these years? How is it that someone to whom words matter greatly finds herself using one she has not planned to use, and of which she does not altogether approve? And using it as a means of addressing someone else to whom words also have mattered greatly, whose chief delight has been their careful deployment in the study of literature?

I don't call him *Baby* all the time, I notice. I notice that I only use it when I am correcting him. I think I'm unconsciously expressing the new fact of our reorientation toward each other—the last time I had to explain how the world worked, it was to my children. I was the Mommy then. As we turn toward the setting sun, I struggle to discern who I am now, and I seize upon a paradigm from earlier in my own life.

Of course it doesn't fit us. There are important differences between my husband and my children of yesteryear. I had a teaching responsibility to them that I do not have to him—I don't have to teach him anything. I am not preparing him for life in the world—he has already lived life in the world. It doesn't matter if he gets something wrong. All that matters is that he has a good moment in the present. And then another, and another. As many as I can help him have.

We are still partners. Most of the inside jokes still work. Our private dialect continues to hold, for the most part. When I notice that a phrase from it has disappeared from our lexicon, I consign it with regret to the dustbin of history. *That was then. This is now.*

These days, I read a lot of books like the one you are about to begin. I want to know how others have made this journey. I need wisdom. I need to learn how to look at life together in ways other than with the lens I've always used. I can do this. But I need help.

Writers like priest and chaplain Colette Bachand-Wood have had the courage and the compassion to offer words of encouragement to those of us still on the long journey of caregiving. Her breadth of chaplaincy experience, in particular, sets the loneliness of our task in a more universal context: others have done this. I am not alone. I may not be able to untie the knot of dementia, but there are concrete things I can do to make this moment better than it would be if I did not do them. For now, this will have to be enough.

And *for now* is all any of us really have.

Barbara Cawthorn Crafton

Introduction

———◆·◆·◆———

Gideon was beating out wheat in the wine press, to hide it from the Midianites. The angel of the LORD appeared to him and said to him, "The LORD is with you, you mighty warrior." Gideon answered him, "But sir, if the LORD is with us, why then has all this happened to us? And where are all his wonderful deeds that our ancestors recounted to us, saying, 'Did not the LORD bring us up from Egypt?' But now the LORD has cast us off, and given us into the hand of Midian." Then the LORD turned to him and said, "Go in this might of yours and deliver Israel from the hand of Midian; I hereby commission you." He responded, "But sir, how can I deliver Israel? My clan is the weakest in Manasseh, and I am the least in my family." The LORD said to him, "But I will be with you . . . ." (Judges 6:11a–16a)

Gideon asks age-old questions: "Why then has all this happened to us?" and "How am I going to get through?"

Three months before my father died from dementia, I got a German Shepherd puppy and I named him Gideon. Having taken strength from this Biblical ancestor who often felt God was asking too much of him, I hoped calling the puppy's name each day would give me some courage. "How can I deliver Israel?" Gideon asks, "I am the least in my family." Gideon, too, often felt insecure and unequipped for the task.

Shortly before Gideon came along, as a family we had made the difficult decision to place my dad in a nursing home. The dementia had progressed to a point we couldn't care for him at home anymore and I somehow felt like I had failed him. To contend with my feelings of helplessness, I needed a distraction and, well, there is nothing like a puppy to distract. They are happy, full of life, need lots of care, and give back lots of love. Gideon was going to be my daily reminder to trust that what felt out of control and impossible might somehow be ok. As Dad's dementia marched on and death ultimately arrived, Gideon was a constant reminder to trust God and seek God's presence. Gideon is now 105 pounds of trust, and when he tries to sit in my lap—which he does often—I can *really* feel God's presence.

My interest in dementia diseases began more than twenty-five years ago when I moved into an apartment with my husband where his old great-aunt Mary lived upstairs. In exchange for a reduced rent we would help care for Mary who was ninety-two at the time. In retrospect, Mary probably had undiagnosed dementia for a very long time. As I watched her and interacted with her, I realized that I needed to do so in ways that were different. I loved being with her: long cups of tea and biscuits, which were just horrible but I ate them anyway, funny little gifts left on my stoop, stories that went in circles and never really ended. A tiny wiry little lady, she walked faster than most people I've ever known. She got hit by city buses, vans backing out on to the street, and fell off curbs and stairs more times than we could count. She always bounced back, and would be on to her next escapade.

One afternoon I came up to her apartment to bring her some leftover dinner from the night before and she was sitting at the kitchen table crying. "Did you hear?" she asked. "The president has been shot and is dead." Although it had been almost three decades since President Kennedy had been assassinated, something triggered her memory and she was reliving it. So I sat and listened to how great a man she thought he was and what a sad day it was for the country. Mary stayed at home for almost all of her life until we kept finding her lighting fires in her kitchen to burn old notes and bills she didn't want anyone to see.

Many years later as I began my ministry career as a chaplain and Episcopal priest, I began meeting more and more people with dementia and their families. When I worked as a hospice chaplain, I would meet these people at the end of their lives and their families would have so many stories to tell. So I began keeping notes and wrote their stories down. I began experimenting with what worked and didn't work in ministry with those with dementia. I eventually left hospice to serve in parish ministry, but continued to work as chaplain in a senior living facility that has a memory care unit. Over time I discovered what a special and needed ministry this was. I attended training classes on caring for people with dementia, researched, attended lectures on Alzheimer's, and developed a specialized worship service geared toward those with memory impairment. In the middle of all this my dad was diagnosed and the journey became personal.

So I've tried to put seven years of stories and research together in a meaningful way that is easy to read and easy to implement.

What you will find in *Do This, Remembering Me* is mostly a collection of stories about people. They are all true stories, some of the names have been changed to provide anonymity, but they are true accounts of where moments of spiritual care have made a difference. Some are funny, some might make you teary, but all are meant to teach and offer a simple message: God is still present and the person with dementia is still alive inside. As God commissioned Gideon, so too does God commission all of us as spiritual caregivers and as family members, to think about the spiritual needs of those who live with dementia.

Whether you are clergy, chaplain, lay spiritual leader, or family member, I hope you will read all parts of the book. While there are some sections with special information for different groups, much overlaps and you may find tools to use for your situation. My hope is that in five or ten years this book will need to be revised because of growing information and treatment. And my hope is that some day, no one will need this book at all as cures are found and preventions discovered.

The title *Do This, Remembering Me* has many meanings. It does of course conjure up images of Holy Eucharist, a time of shared meal, of mystery, of community, and an offering of love. The word "remember" honors what those with Alzheimer's and dementia are living with, it asks us to remember them, and it reminds us that God has not forgotten them.

And finally, the words "Do This." This is the imperative, the invitation, the commissioning, the calling, to in fact take what you learn from these stories and "do this." Do this . . . in *His* memory . . . the one who taught us to love and care for one another. We serve others in Christ's name—and this caring for those with dementia—this we do, in remembrance of Him. Like the promise to Gideon, God will be with us.

CHAPTER ONE

Then Sings My Soul

Listen to me, O house of Jacob,
    all the remnant of the house of Israel,
who have been borne by me from your birth,
    carried from the womb;
even to your old age I am he,
    even when you turn gray I will carry you.
I have made, and I will bear;
    I will carry and will save. (Isaiah 46:3–4)

The first time it happened I cried, then laughed, then asked myself, "What just happened?" The first time a patient with Alzheimer's made a spiritual connection in my presence—moving out of darkness into light, moving out of loneliness into togetherness, moving out of despair into calm—I knew I had witnessed something miraculous, and I was hooked. Thus began a journey to learn how to provide spiritual care to those with Alzheimer's and dementia. God was "still there" for them and I was determined to find ways to help them "remember" the One who calls them beloved. These are some of my first teachers, through whom God spoke. God said, "Pay attention, they have much to teach." And so I listened.

Meet Frank

T'was the week before Christmas and all through the nursing home . . . it was very depressing.

I sat with Frank in a small, outdated common room. Another resident slept soundly in a chair across the room by a window. The hallways were lined with wheelchairs, the air was warm and stale, and a TV in the corner was on but the sound mute. Attempts to decorate the room to look festive had been tried, but the plastic poinsettias struck me as tacky. They were old with branches bent out of shape from being stuffed in a box since last year. There was a Christmas tree in a corner whose lights blinked on and off. I pulled up a chair next to Frank. He looked as though someone had stuffed him in the wheelchair. Food stains covered the front of his shirt; his head was wedged between two pillows. He barely responded when I said, "Hi."

Frank had advanced dementia. A year ago when I visited him, he could recite the Lord's Prayer, take Communion, and tell brief stories about his family and his career as a police officer. So much had changed since then. The times of praying "Our Father" had ceased. No longer at home with his wife of some sixty years, Frank was in this facility where he mostly slept, which was what he was doing that day.

As is so common attempting a pastoral visit with someone with dementia, I had a heavy feeling in my stomach of not knowing what to do with Frank. I felt helpless and even questioned my efforts. Maybe some of the nurses here were right; they would always say to me, "He has no idea what is going on." I always felt like they were discouraging my visits, and today I was feeling that maybe I had been too idealistic about this, maybe all really was lost by now for Frank. The nurses, after all, must know so much more than I do. As I thought about leaving, the lights of the Christmas tree were flickering in colorful patterns with a kind of urgency that nudged me to think differently and seemed to be asking me to hang in. I tried the Lord's Prayer, and finished it alone without response. I sat for some time and held his hand. I sat some more. It was three days before Christmas; I wondered what he was missing out on at home. What did the family do for traditions? Is he missing his favorite warm pumpkin bread? What toy trains had he put together as a young father? Did he teach the kids to ride a bike, "Look Dad, no hands!" Did he dance in the kitchen with his wife?

Today he just slept. And I sat. And then the Christmas tree nudged me again with its insistent lights. So I began to sing. (I will only sing with dementia patients, because I sing very badly, but they never tell anyone.) So I began, *"Silent Night . . . Holy Night . . . All is calm"* . . . and a voice joined me, slow and weak, but precise . . . *"all is bright, round yon virgin, mother and child."* It was Frank and he finished every line of "Silent Night." Though everything else had failed him, his faith remained. *"Sleep in heavenly peace . . . sleep in heavenly peace,"* Frank concluded that day.

Frank died just days after Christmas surrounded by his family. While it might have been easy to imagine that everything had been erased from his memory, in the days before his death it appears "Silent Night" had remained loud and clear.

Meet Dotty

Dotty rambled on like no one else I had ever visited: short quick sets of words like "mother came," "garden water," "go, go, get." Her nursing home room was cheerful and sun splashed; her family had taken obvious efforts to make her comfortable. Along with family pictures, her room was decorated with numerous crucifixes, statuary, and rosary beads. Fresh flowers were on the windowsill, and they had placed her chair so that she could look out the window onto the nursing home's beautifully landscaped grounds.

On my visit that day, I took down the rosary beads and, placing them along Dotty's hands, attempted to say the Hail Mary, but it didn't work. Though I am mostly a stranger to her, just the friendly hospice chaplain, she seemed to only want to hold my hand and, well, sometimes hand-holding is enough. So I held her hand, looking at all the old black-and-white photos on her nightstand. After a while though, I began wishing for something to do with her and I remembered that I had my communion kit with me, having just visited another patient who generally takes communion. For lack of anything else to do, I started to unpack the kit.

I used her bedside tray as a "mock altar" and slowly and quietly "set the table" as I would the altar in church. I laid out my beautiful white linen, my battery-operated candle, a small cross, and a miniature silver chalice and paten. I didn't say anything as I set the altar, just moved slowly, deliberately. She watched me through the corner of her eye. Then suddenly, midway through a ramble about her mother, Dotty stopped talking and got quiet. Dotty was never quiet, so I didn't know what was happening, but then she looked at my altar, took the small chalice in both her hands, lifted it to heaven, and said, very clearly, "Remember me."

Remember indeed!

Meet Allie

I visited Allie at the nursing home one afternoon when I was researching how those with memory impairment responded to visual cues of faith. Allie was a cheerful woman in her nineties and couldn't have weighed more than eighty pounds. Her family had said she was a woman of deep faith and would probably enjoy saying some prayers.

To visit with Allie, I had brought colorful pictures of Jesus, several kinds of crosses, candles, even a Russian stacking doll of the Holy Family. I had church hymns playing on a CD player I had brought in . . . *"Amazing Grace, how sweet the sound . . . ."* I showed Allie a child's picture book of Bible stories with bright colors of Noah's Ark, sheep and the Good Shepherd, angels on high. She didn't respond much to the pictures. I tried to begin prayer, making the sign of the cross: *"In the name of the Father, and of the Son . . . ,"* but Allie didn't follow along and was more interested in the hem of her sweatshirt.

I then took out a beautiful silver cross to show Allie. I didn't say anything; I just let Allie touch it. It was cold from having been out in my car trunk all night. After turning the cross this way and that, Allie paused. A strange look came over her face that turned into a silly, somewhat coy, smile. It seemed to me she was remembering something very pleasant. And suddenly Allie exclaimed excitedly, looking at the cross, "Yes, all that and regular sex too!"

Well, I will never know (and perhaps don't want to know) what Allie remembered that day, but by the look on her face it was a very happy and pleasant memory. When I relayed this story to a colleague, she reminded me that in pious Catholic families of Allie's era, they would have had a crucifix hanging over their bed. They would have knelt by the bedside to say bedtime prayers and probably blessed themselves before getting into bed. Hmmm? God's grace is indeed amazing.

God Does Not Forget

What I learned from Frank, Dotty, Allie, and the numerous other adults with memory loss I've had the privilege to care for, is that for people of faith, Alzheimer's and dementia cannot erase God's imprint. When everything else is crumbling around them, God remains intact and is very present. This makes complete sense because faith has always been something only understood with the heart and not the head. Faith has never made sense on an intellectual level and has never been something to be reasoned or explained with words. Faith is etched in the heart and spirit, so it only stands to reason that dementia cannot rob people of God and their faith. While the disease steals many things, I am convinced that the presence of a loving, healing God is "remembered" and is very real to those with memory loss. After all, one does not need words to know God.

As people of faith, as spiritual caregivers, and as family members who care about our loved ones, providing a space for spirituality and religious practices during the phases of Alzheimer's and dementia is more than just a nice thing to do. As Christians and followers of Jesus, are we not led by his longing to care for "the least of these"? In Jesus's time, the least of these were the poor, the out-casts, and the widows. In our time, those living with memory loss are the new "least of these" that we are called to serve. Throughout the Bible we meet a God who has a special concern for those who were forgotten and suffering. For our generation, in a time, world, and culture that places so much value on youthfulness and pro-ductivity, those of older years and limited ability can be easily for-gotten. But we must not forget them or we lose the very essence of what it means to be a people of hope and healing.

Teepa Snow is a dementia-care specialist, educator, and occupa-tional therapist who has been working with and studying the field of dementia care for over thirty years. She is founder of Positive Approach[1] and travels nationally and internationally teaching fami-lies and nursing home staff how to effectively work with this popu-lation in a way that is nurturing. As spiritual caregivers, Teepa says we have an opportunity to help people address their feelings and deal with the challenges of dementia by reconnecting them with their faith. Through worship and prayer, which naturally draws out emotions, she says spiritual care offers them a place to remember who they still are inside.

For years, she says, people, including clergy, have assumed there was nothing they could do to connect with and reach people with dementia, but her research has proven that wrong. There is always what she calls a "spirit part" inside every person: no matter how far the disease has progressed, there lives a flame that if we can touch will bloom. As providers of spiritual care, according to Teepa, we become not care *givers* but care *partners,* which can enfold them into a larger sense of community and wholeness. She believes

1. www.teepasnow.com

people can be trained to work with dementia patients in a way that is positive, focusing not on their losses but on their abilities. In other words, what can they still do? How can they still be in relationship with people they love? How can their lives be improved through the right kind of care? And so what we have learned is that what they *can* still do is pray, sing, and worship.

Some research on Alzheimer's suggests that people living with dementia often know what they want to communicate but can't use words, especially in the early stages of the disease. So while their "intake" works, their "output" does not: they cannot find the words to communicate back, so we assume "they are gone." I think of all the times in the early stages of my dad's disease that he would word search for a long time and then finally give up. Sometimes he would laugh at himself and point to his head, indicating something wasn't working; it was kind of cute and funny. But sometimes he would get mad and sad. Realizing that *he* knew what was happening to him was heartbreaking for us, his family.

When I think about this, I try to imagine what it would be like to be trapped in a body and mind that knows what it needs, wants, and longs for, but can't ask for. And then I imagine the chaplain, my parish priest, my friend, or my spouse coming in, treating me as though I *am* still there, praying out loud words I ache to speak myself, letting there be a quiet moment where I can ask God for help too, and then singing *"Joyful, joyful, we adore thee."* What a difference this would make in my life when others are merely rolling me over in bed to change my Depends, forcing me to sit in chairs I don't want to sit in, and talking to me like I am a child. It is amazing care to give. Whether in the form of a prayer, a song, or a shared moment of tears, this ministry validates that those with dementia are still alive inside.

I was once invited to attend an Alzheimer's caregiver support group at the agency where I was working as the hospice chaplain. Some of those gathered were family of patients I'd been visiting. After I demonstrated some of the things that I do with patients, I noticed one of the women at the far end of the table was crying. I stopped and said, "Would it be ok if I asked what has triggered your tears?" She said, "Thank you for doing this, everyone else has given up on them."

When I play the hymn "How Great Thou Art" during my service of "Prayers and Song" in the memory care unit, I notice that people with otherwise few words will suddenly sing very loud and clear the refrain, *"Then sings my soul, my savior Lord to thee, how great thou art."* The souls of those with Alzheimer's and dementia indeed do still sing. No matter how advanced the disease, faith is not lost and we will do well to "Do This, Remembering Me."

Interlude

My Huckleberry Friend

It might have been his last "professional" appearance.

I had come for a visit to his memory care unit and as I walked down the hall past Dad's room (he was never in his room), I noticed he was sitting next to Mary, and Mary was clearly in the midst of a good cry. As she sobbed, overwhelmed by some sadness she couldn't speak, Mary sniffled loudly and big tears ran down her red face.

Dad had one hand on Mary's arm and in the other he held a clipboard. In language only dementia patients share, it appeared he was giving her some advice, some council. Most likely it was legal advice, which he had spent his lifetime giving people as a lawyer and city councillor. As Dad sat with Mary, he was being intentional with his words and looked very much the part of "attorney extraordinaire"— serious, compassionate, and ready to take notes with his clipboard. He had that "leaning forward, making a point" body language I had seen in his younger years when he tried to explain the legal ramifications of some thing. This is the man who dealt with racial riots and urban growth, defended a family whose daughter had been burned by flammable pajamas, and stood by fishermen trying to make a living in our hometown of New Bedford, Massachusetts, a city known for its once vibrant fishing industry.

That morning in the memory care unit, it was easy, for a moment, to see Dad as he used to be; to imagine him not a patient here, but rather, the facility's legal expert come to help. It was easy, for a moment, to see him as he had once been: well dressed, gentle and gentleman, wise attorney and confidant who could ease whatever your worry.

It *would* have been easy to imagine all these things . . . except . . . he was wearing a straw hat decorated with huge colorful silk flowers.

An aide finally came over to assist Mary in her despair, so I tried to distract Dad. "Nice hat," I said, but he didn't connect my words with the cartoon-like thing on his head—the hat in complete opposition to his very serious face.

We were lucky; Dad's dementia never took away his ability to recognize family. Sometimes he confused us, like calling his son his brother's name, but for the most part, he knew who we were and was always happy to see us.

After the aide took Mary away, Dad and I walked down the hall. He was a walker, always pacing—I think that is how he and Mary became friends; she was a walker too. After lap two around the unit, I asked if he wanted to take the straw hat off. He said he would keep it on. (There are some things you don't argue over with dementia patients, colorful straw hats being one of them.)

As we headed to the music room where I knew a singer was performing, I had Dad stop in the bathroom, "Hey, look how cute you are in the hat," I told him steering him in the direction of the mirror.

He looked at himself, laughed, and then made the silly face that had become his trademark since dementia freed him from his otherwise serious self. His goofy face made me laugh too, and when I laughed he said, "Hey, don't laugh at me, I'm your father."

When those very "clear" full sentences came out, it was always bittersweet. Bitter because as family it made me worry he knew more and understood more than we thought; but then sweet too, because I knew he remembered I was daddy's little girl. It was always nice to have a little of him back, even if for a short time.

We walked into the room where an entertainer was singing, "*I did it my way.*" Heads of the aides turned as Dad walked in the room still in the straw hat. We took a seat side by side. He was his usual self for the next few songs, listening to the music one moment, tapping his knees and clapping, then, in the next moment, asking questions about things I couldn't piece together, and so to which I offered, "I'm not really sure." This had become a customary answer to questions that didn't make sense. Other responses I had learned were things like, "I'll have to check on that" or "I'll look into it." These usually worked well, especially when he seemed exceptionally worried or concerned about something.

As we sat listening, I was thinking to myself that I wanted to remember to write down the scene I had just witnessed with Dad and Mary in the notebook of "cute stories" I'd been keeping about him and other dementia patients. For over a year I had been jotting down sayings, stories, and observations I wanted to remember. "The encounter with Mary would be a good addition," I was thinking to myself as the singer moved into a rather nice version of "Moon River" . . . "*Waiting round the bend, my huckleberry friend, Moon River and me.*"

Huckleberry friend . . . I repeated the phrase to myself, thinking it would be a perfect title for the piece about Dad and Mary. He was always such a good friend to her, in his own way, and right now in the hat, he looked like a "huckleberry friend."

Songwriter Johnny Mercer coined the phrase "huckleberry friend" for a song in the old movie *Breakfast at Tiffany's*. Mercer grew up in Savannah, Georgia, and wrote "Moon River" thinking about the waterways of his youth, the huckleberries he picked as a kid, and the connection he found between them and his carefree boyhood of which the character Huckleberry Finn was a hero. Over the years the term has come to evoke a sense of lifelong friendship. Huckleberry friend?

I suddenly felt emotional about the way dad had become my huckleberry friend too. Over the last years in his dementia, I'd gotten to know him in a way I otherwise wouldn't have. Growing up he was the consummate 1960s, 1970s dad, working two jobs, involved in church and civic life, who loved sports on Sunday afternoons and was always home for dinner. But dads of his generation weren't hands-on like modern dads; we didn't spend a lot of time together outside of family time, but his dementia brought something new. We got to spend a lot of time together. I got to know him in helping to care for him, differently, tenderly, simply—quiet cups of coffee, silent walks, hand-holding, looking over old photos, and from time to time, hearing pieces from stories of long, long ago. Sometimes I got the sense he trusted me, but with what and about what I don't know. He didn't get agitated when I was around, and when it was just the two of us, he was calm and peaceful.

Listening to "Moon River," I rubbed the back of his neck and noticed how he smelled, clean but somehow institutional, like disinfectant or something. I wondered if everyone in the room smelled the same way. I had to fight back the pit in my stomach where the sadness lived, sadness that Dad had to be here and not home with us. As I was thinking all these things, he suddenly started to fidget with something in his pocket and pulled out a stack of white napkins, clean and neatly folded. He looked through them gently, stacking them and then fanning them as one would if looking through pages of a book.

Then he leaned over to me, and taking the napkins as if he was indeed opening a book, he said, very clearly, "Another writing by Colette Bachand."

How could he have known I was thinking about writing about him and Mary? He couldn't have known, I'd never said anything to him about it, ever. But there it was, he *had* said it.

I didn't know at the time, but this would be our last visit where it was just the two of us. It was the last time we would walk down the hall together, giggle in a mirror, talk nonsense, and clap to old songs. In just a few weeks he would be gone, and so would these moments . . . .

Change was indeed just around the bend for my huckleberry friend . . . and me.

CHAPTER TWO

Understanding Alzheimer's and Dementia

You clothed me with skin and flesh,
    and knit me together with bones and sinews.
You have granted me life and steadfast love,
    and your care has preserved my spirit.

                                        (Job 10:11–12)

W e are fortunate to live at a time when so much has been learned about Alzheimer's and dementia. Numerous studies have been and are being done on its causes, medications have been created that can slow its growth, support groups are everywhere for those dealing with the disease, funding to find a cure is ongoing, and testing is even available for children of Alzheimer's patients who might want to know if they carry the gene. Public knowledge and education about Alzheimer's and dementia is growing, and families who once tried to cover up and hide the disease are now living in a much more compassionate and understanding society.

We have a lot of facts too, like these from the Alzheimer's Association.[2] We know that:

- Every 67 seconds, someone in the United States develops Alzheimer's.
- Alzheimer's/dementia is the sixth leading cause of death in the United States.
- In 2013, family and friends of people with dementia provided 18 billion hours of caregiving.
- Women tend to be at the center of the illness: by their late sixties, 1 in 6 women are at risk for developing dementia (compared to 1 in 11 for breast cancer), and women are more likely to be caring for a family member with Alzheimer's than are men.
- While in 2015 there were approximately 5.1 million people in the United States living with Alzheimer's, by the year 2035 that number will reach 9.9 million and by 2050, 13.5 million. That means that, barring a cure, there will be millions of baby boomers who will either have Alzheimer's or will be caring for someone who does.
- In 2015, Alzheimer's and other forms of dementia will cost $226 billion in the United States, going up to $1.1 trillion by 2050.

---

2. www.alz.org/facts/overview.asp

People often use the terms Alzheimer's and dementia interchangeably, and that is easy to do since from a symptoms standpoint, they look very much the same. Alzheimer's, however, is a *form* of dementia, and is the most common form. Most people also think that dementia is a disease of memory loss, but it is so much more than just the loss of memories. It is truly a disease of brain degeneration.

Alzheimer's and other forms of dementia cause many of the same symptoms including cognitive decline and confusion; inability to complete tasks and connect words; changes in mood or personality; and eventually an inability to feed, wash, or toilet on their own. Some maintain their ability to recognize names and faces of loved ones, others do not. Memory losses associated with dementia often find people able to retrieve long-term memories, like the name of a second-grade teacher or an outing with their brother when they were teenagers, but can't recall what they had for lunch or how to put socks on. Sometimes the woman who was kind and sweet throughout her life becomes angry and volatile; sometimes the man who was stern and serious suddenly loves to cuddle and hold hands.

Alzheimer's as a disease is generally broken down into three stages: early or mild, middle to moderate, and severe or late stage. There is no exact science to determine what stage a person is in, and on average a person lives four to eight years after being diagnosed with Alzheimer's, but many can and do live much, much longer.

Following Alzheimer's is vascular dementia as the second most common form of dementia. The medical field now refers to vascular dementia as Vascular Cognitive Impairment (VCI) and it is usually brought on by a major stroke or a series of smaller strokes called TIAs (Transient Ischemic Attacks). Other health issues like high cholesterol, high blood pressure, or other blood vessel diseases can cause VCI. Dementia can also be triggered by diseases such Parkinson's, Lewy bodies (LBD), and Huntington's Disease, or can be a "mixed" dementia in which memory loss and brain failure comes from multiple factors. Some dementias can be treated and cognitive capabilities improved, especially if related to less permanent medical conditions. Alzheimer's, however, worsens over time, has no cure, and is caused by nerve damage in the brain usually associated with "plagues" and "tangles" that cause nerve cells to die.

While doctors can use MRIs and other tests to pinpoint whether someone has Alzheimer's, VCI, or other dementias, some families never know for sure what has caused someone's memory loss and decline. Some people may want to know and understand all the medical and scientific components of dementia, and some will want to confirm an Alzheimer's diagnosis for future family members, but many may just want to know how to best live with the disease and its symptoms.

Caring for Those with Dementia

Learning to live and work with people with dementia will be critical in our ministries of the future because dementia does not happen in isolation. Its impact stretches far and wide and changes the face of families, congregations, neighborhoods, and other places where people gather. Fortunately there are many now working to better the lives of people with dementia, trying to make a positive impact by using music to calm, training nursing home staff in positive care techniques, and integrating care to include holistic treatments like meditation, exercise, and art therapy.

How we act and interact with people with dementia will greatly impact the outcome of the lives we share with them. Just as we are fortunate to live when there is a great deal of knowledge about dementia diseases, we also live at a time when we can learn from others' experiences of ways of positive techniques for caregiving. We can learn, for example, how to de-escalate confrontations, how to (and how not to) calm someone who is worked up and upset, and how to get them to do the tasks needed to be done, like eating, feeding, and washing. We can learn to communicate better with the person with dementia in ways that are compassionate and validating rather than demeaning or impersonal. We all have a tendency to want to make people feel better and will make the mistake of telling someone who has dementia and might be sad, mad, and angry all at the same time, "It's ok, don't worry," and then we wonder why they have become suddenly agitated and uncooperative. When we say things like "It is ok and don't worry," I imagine that if they could they would just scream that it is *not* ok, and they *are* worried, they have dementia and the world is slipping away from them. Rephrasing our statements to sound something more like, "This must be so frustrating," or "I can see this really angers you," or "This must be so hard" can create positive communications and prevent upsets.

Teepa Snow (of Positive Approach mentioned earlier) teaches how something as simple as body language can aid our interactions with the person with dementia. She demonstrates how greeting someone with a simple handshake and then moving to stand side by side with them, while still holding their hand, puts us in a partnership relationship, rather than a confrontational one standing face to face. She teaches how to deal with anger and rage, what to do when the person with dementia has gotten so worked up they are yelling and swearing. Most of us will try to calm them or redirect them, but this can be a challenge. The person with dementia wants to and needs to be in interpersonal relationships and since they can no longer control the dimensions of those relationships, it is up to us to join them where they are.

There are so many skills and tools to use in caring for those with dementia that even someone whose goal it is to provide spiritual care might also want to have some of these tricks of the trade. What a clever pastor you will seem when your parishioner is sharing with you her frustrations over her husband's bathroom struggles and you suggest she use a colorful toilet seat. (For men this helps them figure out where to aim; colors are always helpful tools since their vision changes.) Other things you could know about are things like putting a black rubberized rug in front of a door to discourage wandering (again, because of vision changes, the black rug looks like a hole), or putting colorful pictures up around the house (or nursing home room) to help them remember where to put things (like a picture of eye glasses on a nightstand to help them remember where to leave them for the morning). Many people might not yet know that there are now even safety devices like GPS bracelets that people with dementia can wear in case they wander.

It is so easy to feel helpless in the midst of living with, working with, or ministering to someone with dementia. And while so much feels lost, there is still so much we can do together, we just have to learn how to do it differently and change our expectations.

Interlude

Honesty

There are some things that are just inevitable when it comes to living with and ministering to people with Alzheimer's and dementia. Unfortunately, failures, flops, and frustrations are among them. Here are some examples from both my experiences with my dad as well as experiences in ministry where things didn't work out exactly as I had hoped. Whether you are a family member trying to create religious moments for your loved one or whether you are clergy or staff at a facility, accepting that pastoral care is not an exact science, will be evermore important when working with people with dementia. In the long run, the magical moments when we say, "Wow, that was wonderful!" will far outnumber the more difficult ones, I promise. If a visit feels like a failure, just do as Jesus did: Shake off the dust from your shoes, and keep trying.

Failure

Dad had only been in the nursing home for a few days when I decided I would try to do prayer and communion with him. He was lying in bed when I got there, which should have been my first clue. He was a walker, a pacer, so for him to be lying down wasn't normal, but I wasn't being smart or paying attention to his body language. I should have just sat and said and done nothing, but I was intent on trying to find some way of making this situation better. (Or was I, perhaps, trying to make myself feel better?) Moving him to a nursing home felt miserable, like a betrayal, like we had given up on him. I wanted so much to make things better, so in I marched to his room determined to fix everything. I got out my prayer book and my communion kit; I began some prayers and suddenly he just started to cry with a look on his face that was of such terror and confusion that I became terrified and confused myself. Panicking, and with my own emotions out of control, I stupidly offered him communion, which he choked on. I put the headboard of his bed up higher and waited for him to catch his breath.

What was I thinking? When he stopped choking, I just put everything away. He wasn't ready for the emotional feelings that come with prayers. He had only been there three days and was already on emotional overload about everything . . . unable to understand why he was there, surrounded by people he didn't know, afraid and feeling abandoned. I should have just sat, but I had *my* agenda. What was I thinking? So I did what I should have done in the first place, just held his hand. And cried too.

Frustration

I have learned you can't look back.

And I don't mean in the metaphorical sense of not being able to look back to better days. I mean literally, you can't look back when you drop him off at the nursing home. You can't look back because if you do, you'll make eye contact again and the whole struggle will start over. The struggle with him asking: Why he has to stay, why can't he come home with you, what is he supposed to do? And then the struggle will start again within yourself asking: Why does he have to stay, why he can't come home with me, what is he supposed to do?

So don't look back. When you leave, keep walking, even if he is watching you from inside the glass doors. Don't wave that one last time like you did when he dropped you off at college or when he walked you to the car with his new granddaughter in his arms. There can't be that one last wave that has an unspoken assurance we will see each other again, soon. The wave doesn't work anymore. He already seems gone.

Flops

Some visits with Alzheimer's patients are just flops and can be quite humorous. Here are two flop stories from my past.

The first was with a hospice patient who was living in a nursing home. Her family said she was very religious and would respond well to a visit. With my bag packed, off I went and found her lying in bed looking out the window. She seemed comfortable, warmly bundled in blankets, with a calm look on her face. I stepped around the side of the bed, smiled as big as I could and introduced myself, slowly offering a hand to shake. She didn't take my hand. I said I was the chaplain and had brought my prayers with me. Her stare was a blank, but then her face got all twisted up and after a few seconds became red, red, red and she screamed out loud, "Get out of here before I kill you!"

I said something like, "Oh, honey, I just thought we might pray together" and I began Psalm 23 (sometimes starting the prayer makes it easier for them to know what you want to do and why you are there, not to change a diaper or force a pill down but to pray). I made the sign of the cross and said, "The Lord is my shepherd . . . ." But she screamed, "Get out or I'll kill you!" So I left the room and waited about fifteen minutes in the hallway. Sometimes just waiting and trying again helps, so yes, I hoped that she had forgotten I was just there, but when I returned it was the same thing. At this point I took my bag and left. This is her life, her terms, her agenda, not mine, and not her family's who had wanted her to have a visit from the chaplain. At least not today.

The other story has to do with Psalm 23 as well and another nursing home patient. I had seen this woman before and prayer time always went well. Today when I arrived though, all she kept saying was, "I have to pee, I have to pee." She was bedbound and couldn't get to the bathroom on her own. I did try and find an aide to help, but couldn't find anyone so assured her I would look again when our prayers were over. She was fidgety, not engaging in the "ritual" as she usually did, and our time together came to an abrupt end when, as I was reciting, "You have anointed my head with oil and my cup runneth over," she blurted out, "If someone doesn't come soon, *my* cup is going to runneth over." I laughed so much I couldn't continue. It was a full, clear sentence. I decided to forget the prayers and just sit with her while we waited for help. Sometimes spiritual care is just waiting together for a bathroom run.

CHAPTER THREE

Spiritus

———————

Breathe on me, Breath of God,
    fill me with life anew,
that I may love what thou dost love,
    and do what thou wouldst do.[3]

S tories paint such beautiful pictures, and people with
dementia have so many stories to tell. Those who work
with this population can tell you of the miracles, the "aha"
moments and celebrations that happen when ministering among
people with dementia. Grand moments when there has been a
connection, when a hymn has brought someone back, and when
faith has been remembered. They are joyous stories and they exist

---

3. "Breathe on me, Breath of God," *The Hymnal 1982* (New York: Church
Hymnal, 1982), hymn 508.

alongside the tough stories: stories of brilliant college professors now mute and unable to feed themselves; stories of mothers once full of life, making big holiday dinners and at the center of family life, now unable to remember the faces of those she loves.

I would like to share with you a few stories about this ministry from others who provide spiritual care to those with Alzheimer's and dementia. They are gathered from others who work as chaplains, priests, and laypeople either in nursing homes or memory care units. In these stories you will witness something profound, small moments when those who seem to be living in darkness are brought out of the dark and for a moment, *sometimes ever so brief,* shine with the light of God as they reconnect. These are folks who are "doing this, remembering Him."

Meet Paul

Stan is chaplain at a senior living facility in Massachusetts where he works in the memory care unit. (His name and the patients' have been changed.) Stan talks about the special experiences he has during a weekly worship service he calls the "Hymn Sing" in which residents gather to sing traditional church songs. Instead of recorded music, Stan is blessed to have piano accompaniment from a man named Paul, who is a resident in the facility. Paul is a retired minister, lover of church music, and Paul has dementia. Because of his disease, Paul cannot find his way to the facility's chapel or back to his room if it weren't for his wife. Paul cannot find page numbers in the worship book without help. For Paul, conversations are difficult and diminishing. There are many things Paul cannot do now because of dementia, but the minute Paul's old hymnal is placed in front of him, something reconnects. Paul is able to play each song beautifully and participate fully in the worship service.

Despite his dementia, Paul is still Paul. At some point in his life he chose ministry because he wanted to love and serve God's people. Paul didn't stop being a minister when he got dementia. By playing music for the hymn sing, Paul continues his ministry, he remembers the music, and there is a connection dementia cannot steal. His dignity and self-worth are maintained and he is made to feel of value.

Meet Ella

Of all the people who come to the Hymn Sing, there was once a woman named Ella who Stan was very fond of and who has since passed away. Ella was one of the few Jewish residents in the building and was in the late stages of dementia when she attended Stan's service. She was very withdrawn, noncommunicative, and minimally responsive to words. The Hymn Sing was predominately Christian, so when Ella started attending, Stan changed his format so that there was a "Hebrew Interlude."

Stan tells how Ella would be wheeled into the service and would sleep through "The Old Rugged Cross" and other Christian hymns. Right before the Hebrew music would begin, Stan would get very close to Ella and say, "Shalom." "Shalom was her wake-up word," Stan said. "She would wake up, eyes open, beaming, and be fully alive, if only for a few moments. Often there was even a hug involved. By the end of the music she was gone again."

"Shalom" means so many things and has deep meaning in the Jewish faith. In Hebrew communities, friends and family greet each other and bid farewell with the word. Shalom means peace, completeness, well-being, soundness. Shalom has attachments to names for the Divine. As I thought about Stan's story of Ella, it occurred to me there was no coincidence Shalom was her "wake-up word."

> For the mountains may depart
>   and the hills be removed,
> but my steadfast love shall not depart from you,
>   and my covenant of peace shall not be removed,
>   says the LORD, who has compassion on you. (Isaiah 54:10)

Dementia may shake the mountains and rattle the hills, but God's love, and peace, is unfailing.

Meet Henry

The Reverend Tom Davis is an American Baptist minister and chaplain at a senior living facility in Memphis, Tennessee. Davis is part of the new movement in caring for people with dementia created by the nonprofit called "Music & Memory,"[4] which is working with families and care facilities around the country to put iPods into the hands of people with Alzheimer's and dementia. The iPods contain a playlist with the person's favorite music, the idea being that music can muster up memories and the emotions attached to them. Nursing homes experimenting with the iPods are finding that residents are calmer, more peaceful, and easier to redirect. From a physiological standpoint, the patients also show improved physical symptoms like a slower heartbeat and lower blood pressure.

---

4. http://musicandmemory.org

"Music frees the whole brain, it can be like a rewiring device," says Davis. One of his residents regained "expressive speech"— the ability to talk and respond—after use of the iPod, despite having been mute and unresponsive for years. With the help of the patient's daughter, Davis created a playlist of songs from the 50s and 70s which he had been told were her favorites. Within a short time of listening to the iPod, the patient began to make sounds, then giggle, then sing, and eventually over time speak in partial sentences, including using people's names. Davis would take the resident to the chapel from time to time where she would sit with her daughter and listen to hymns on the iPod, an experience that allowed the mother and daughter to mend some of the broken relationship and heal some of the past.

Davis also points to the Music & Memory website, which tells the story of Henry who loves music and has very advanced dementia. Henry had been in a nursing home for a decade and had completely withdrawn, was uncommunicative and unengaged until he got his iPod. Loaded with religious music and jazz from his era, the iPod drew Henry out of his dark place. Now, when staff put on his music, Henry sways in his wheelchair, sings out loud, and when the music is removed, for a short time, answers questions with appropriate, if not inspiring, answers.

In the video,[5] Henry is asked what listening to the music does for him and answers that he "feels the love." He uses other phrases too, like "I feel a band of love" and even adds, "The Lord . . . gave me these sounds." He then goes on to be-bop like Cab Calloway and sings, *"I'll be home for Christmas,"* eyes wide and a smile even

_____

5. www.youtube.com/watch?v=fyZQf0p73QM&list=UUWSW0VyPUvG 8dfJc9VtFQRg

wider. Through the right care, Henry is restored to who he has always been. Henry is Henry again . . . and still. The flame inside of him has been rekindled, the God who loves him felt present. After listening to the music, Henry tells the interviewer that God has made him a holy man. Holy indeed, holy and blessed, and remembered.

If secular music can create such well-being for people, church music can double that effect. "It is said singing hymns is like praying twice," said Davis, "so for people to be able to listen to their favorite church music holds great potential." He says so many patients with the disease are confined to wheelchairs and often sit alone for long periods of time. By placing a headset on them with old church hymns, they are no longer alone; they have reconnected with God and with memories.

Along with music, Davis uses forms of centering prayer, *lectio divina*, the Jesus prayer, Anglican prayer beads, and other "contemplative" spiritual practices to calm residents and redirect them when they are agitated. He believes the goal of spiritual care providers (including family members) should be first to ask not *what* spiritual care a person should have, but rather ask what spiritual *pain* the person might be in. By the time someone comes into a nursing home or is homebound being cared for with this disease, they have already suffered a great deal of trauma due to significant losses. This is especially true when someone has been placed in a facility.

"When trauma happens, as individuals it is something we have no experience with and no context for how to deal with," says Davis. "When someone has experienced trauma, there are three things that can happen: They run, they fight, and/or they disassociate. Unfortunately this is true when someone is moved into a facility.

They are mad, resistant and they shut down, often leading to mis-diagnosis." And when people are this frightened, he witnesses time and again how music calms a frightened spirit, especially church music when someone is a person of faith. Davis feels our current health care system for those with Alzheimer's and dementia is too geared toward the body and that we need to focus more on the spirit. "A frightened or scared spirit cannot heal or be well," he says.

Meet Ken

Teepa Snow, founder of Positive Approach, tells the story of visiting a memory care unit late one evening when she came across Ken.[6] She observed that Ken seemed very agitated, was walking up and down the hall, pacing, and seemed in distress. After watching him for a short time, she caught up to him, hooked her arm in his, and started to say, "Oh, oh, oh!" in a distressing manner. Teepa explains that she was trying to give expression to what it appeared he was feeling. She kept walking with him, and repeating, "Oh, oh" and then started saying, "I hate this, I hate this, I hate this!" Teepa says she was not only trying to give expression to his body language, but trying to "join" him in the distress he was feeling. The goal she said was to meet him where he was.

"Far too often we try to bring people to where *we* want them to be," she said. As caregivers of people with dementia, we want to make them feel better so we might do things like try to convince them everything is ok, but she says we do better by assessing what *they* need before jumping in and not being afraid to join them in their discomfort, which is what she was doing with Ken.

---

6. Teepa Snow, interview with author, April 2015.

Teepa continued to pace the hall with Ken that night, moaning and repeating, "I hate this, I hate this." At one point, Ken suddenly stopped. He looked at Teepa and with great clarity said, "I have to go home now. Tell my family I'm sorry, I tried to wait, but I had to go." Ken was calm after that, he went to bed, and by morning Ken had died.

Teepa had provided Ken with the spiritual comfort that he was not alone, that he had been understood, and could die knowing she would say good-bye to his family. Hospice caregivers will tell you when someone knows they are dying, there are generally five things they want, no matter what their disease. The five things are: to say I love you, to hear I love you, to offer forgiveness, to accept forgiveness, and to say good-bye. Snow provided a place where Ken could say good-bye, not by telling him everything would be ok, but by merely being with him in his pain.

The Reverend Doctor Ronald Hindelang is a chaplain and Clinical Pastoral Education supervisor at a major Boston hospital, overseeing the training of students who are studying for careers in ministry. Hindelang often gets questions from his students about how to interact with patients who come into the hospital who have dementia but are there for other reasons like a broken bone or pneumonia.

"I tell them it is much like visiting someone who is in intensive care and may be sedated or unresponsive. I believe that they are still there but can't respond, and so we must reach out to them and there are many things we can do like just sit with them," he says, adding that he believes in the power of presence. "People with dementia can pick up on the compassion I am sending to them. Their spirits can feel the caring energy, and by just being present and not afraid to visit, we witness God's faithful love for them in the middle of what they are going through."[7]

Meet Mazie

And last is my story of Mazie. Mazie seems a little too young to be in a memory care unit, although we know it is becoming more and more common to find people in their fifties and sixties in these facilities. Mazie is little lady with a beautiful smile; a smile that I would guess served her well in life. I imagine she was well liked and fun to be around. But while her smile is beautiful, it has been appearing less and less since I first met her more than a year ago. In the past few months, when I arrive to do my program of hymns and prayers, things are usually going the same for Mazie, which is to say that they are not going well. When I get there she is usually pacing the halls, walking slowly, as if in pain, and usually very distraught. When she sees me, she has taken to bursting into tears, very big sad tears and usually says something like, "Thank God you are here!" After being away one week, she greeted me with, "Oh, it's been awful, just awful."

One afternoon it seemed Mazie was having an especially hard day. When she saw me she started crying, which wasn't too unusual, but she was practically running toward me with her arms wide open. "Hello my friend," I said gently, taking her in my arms. She put her head on my shoulder and started to say that no one has been to visit her, that her back hurt, and she doesn't know where she is supposed to go.

7. Snow, interview.

"Well I've got just the place to go!" I said. "Today is church day, come I'll show you." I could feel the weight of her sadness as we walked together, arms around each other, into the room where I have my service. I showed her the little "altar" I set and said, "Mazie, how about you sit here, right next to me, so we can be together?"

"That would be good," she said, taking the seat that has actually become hers, indeed right next to me, where I can hold her shaky hand.

The others gathered one by one to our little church service. Seated in a circle of chairs and wheelchairs, with the altar at our center, we sang "Amazing Grace" and "How Great Thou Art," we prayed the Lord's Prayer, the prayer of St. Francis. Mazie knows all the words and without fail, when our prayer and song time is over, Mazie is a new person. The tears are gone. She is clapping to "This Little Light of Mine," and when I shake her hand and say "God's peace be with you," she answers with complete clarity, "And also with you." Mazie leaves the room smiling, not needing me to walk her out. Each week I have to practically carry her *into* our program, but each week she walks out by herself, heading off to the next activity a different person.

We all know that the word "spirit" in spirituality and spiritual caregiving comes from the Latin *spiritus* for breath. What the stories of Mazie, Ken, Ella, and the others reveal is God's breath still present in them. We provide spiritual care that we might nourish this breath of God, creating moments of Pentecost, when words seemingly inaudible are understood any way.

Interlude

The Dementia Dance

Nothing has changed in Ed and Rose's house since sometime in the 1970s. Impeccably clean and well preserved, their first-floor apartment was frozen in time . . . gold shag carpet, green couch, and wooden furniture with long spindles and simple lines. The only things that seemed to have aged in forty years were Ed and Rose themselves. Ed is in his early 90s now and Rose in her late 80s. They are of a time gone by. They raised four children in this apartment, the same house that Rose herself was born in. They found everything they ever needed right in their own hometown.

Now Rose has dementia.

Ed and Rose were parishioners at a church where I was serving. Having been told by the previous clergy that Rose had dementia, I came to visit, not sure what I would find. After my knock on the door, Rose opened it with a grand smile. She is a beautiful woman with thick white hair, cut into a clean bob, and bright blue eyes. She was neatly dressed and steady on her feet. "Hello," she said, "Can I help you?" I had scheduled the visit with Ed, and whether he had told her I wasn't sure.

I cheerfully said, "Hello, Rose, I am Reverend Colette, the priest from church." She smiled and asked me to come in. So far, she did not appear at all to be someone with dementia, but rather just a kindly old lady you'd expect to offer you chocolate chip cookies and a glass of milk. After she closed the door, however, she didn't seem to know what to do next, which is when Ed appears and invites me into the living room.

Ed is in remarkable shape. Aside from some hearing and vision loss, he is sharp, witty, and engaging. He never offers the information that Rose has dementia, and as we begin talking I watch a dance unfold. Ed and Rose compensate for each other with an elegance and precision that is remarkable. Rose is Ed's ears and eyes, and Ed is Rose's thought and direction. Because he cannot hear well, Rose repeats almost everything I say to him; because she repeats it, he is able to give her the answers.

"She asked how long we have been married," Rose leans closer to Ed, repeating my question, to which he says seventy-one years. "Yes, seventy-one years," Rose smiles, nodding her head as though she had come up with the answer herself.

Ed begins telling me about their activities with the church when they were young and raising a family. Something clicks with Rose while he is talking and she begins to say, "Yes, I did the thing there . . . with the . . . where you put the napkin . . . on top . . . ." She is making hand gestures that clue me in that she is setting up something.

"You were on the altar guild?" Ed nods yes and she looks to him for the answer to my question. "Oh, yes," she says, "that was nice."

Ed tells me more about their lives; about how they met as teenagers hanging out in the local park; how he went off to World War II, and they were married after that. He told how after the war he was stationed in Alaska, and she took a train all by herself from Massachusetts to see him. Nine months later their first child was born, he tells me with a grin. She tells several stories as well, several times. Ed makes no apologies for the repeated stories, nor does he correct her.

After a while I asked if they would like to receive Communion, and it is clear she doesn't know what I mean. She says to Ed, "What do you think?" As he is trying to decide, I begin to unpack my Communion kit on the coffee table. When Rose sees this, the chalice, paten, candle, and cross, her face lights up, "Oh this will be good." The word "Communion" hadn't connected but the visual cues did. We pray, share the bread and wine; she says all of the Lord's Prayer and holds her hands tight together with a gentle smile on her face.

After our prayer, I say I should probably be getting back to the church. "But of course you'd like tea and a raspberry square first," says Ed. I try to politely decline, but when Ed said that he got them because he knew I was coming, I knew I had to stay. Why is my generation always in such a rush, no time for raspberry squares unless it is purchased from some stranger in a drive-through window of a coffee shop? I answer that a raspberry square would be lovely.

We walk into their kitchen, where I noticed three napkins had already been set. When I attempt to cut a square in half before placing it on my napkin, Ed won't hear of it and insists I need to put on weight anyway. Rose devours her square quietly as Ed tells me about his time in the service.

As we are finishing, I say to Ed and Rose that if they want to come to church on Sundays, I would be happy to find someone who could pick them up, that it would be lovely to have them. Perhaps Rose would like being in the church?

"No," Ed says without a second thought. "Everything has changed out there. We only go out on Tuesday mornings when our daughter takes us to the grocery store, pharmacy, or a doctor appointment. We don't know any of the people in town, all the stores are different now, and things aren't where they used to be. No, we are happy right here."

"Then I will be happy to bring church to you," I say, realizing the depth and truth to what he had just said. At home was a world they could navigate. If the phone rang, Ed couldn't hear it but Rose could and knew to bring it to him. At home, he didn't have to explain to anyone why she couldn't finish a sentence. At home she wasn't overwhelmed by sights and sounds she couldn't process. At home, the toaster was where it always was, the bathroom in the very same spot, and the picture of grandma and grandpa from Poland hung where it has always hung. At home, things were as they had always been and that was good enough for them.

The world out there—with mega pharmacies that have replaced family run ones, restaurants now with big-screen TVs and Keno machines everywhere, and coffee shops with a hundred choices of flavored coffees—this is not their world. They are from a time where if you were ordering a coffee, your choices were black or regular.

In marriage ceremonies we speak of couples becoming one. Ed and Rose had literally done this, and even in her dementia, Rose is still the dance partner of the man she waited to return home from war.

CHAPTER FOUR

Faith and Families

———◆◆◆———

Have you not known? Have you not heard?
The Lord is the everlasting God,
    the Creator of the ends of the earth.
He does not faint or grow weary;
    his understanding is unsearchable.
He gives power to the faint,
    and strengthens the powerless.
Even youths will faint and be weary,
    and the young will fall exhausted;
but those who wait for the Lord shall renew
        their strength,
    they shall mount up with wings like eagles,
they shall run and not be weary,
    they shall walk and not faint. (Isaiah 40:28–31)

After years of caregiving for my dad, our family finally found a way to give mom a long needed rest. My brother and I would take turns staying with Dad, and she would go to Cape Cod to stay with family for a little R&R.

My first day with Dad went fine. He came to my house for the afternoon, tossed a ball to our Boston terrier, and had that second cookie that mom never lets him eat at home. (Ok, maybe there was even a third cookie, shh!) We had a simple dinner back at his house and watched a few episodes of "Little House on the Prairie," which had become his favorite show. Feeling pretty exhausted after the day of trying to keep Dad entertained, I proposed it was time to get pajamas on and head to bed.

Dad got as far as his bedroom but then sat down in a chair in protest. I got his pajamas out of the drawer, laid them on the bed, and offered to help him with his slippers. As I reached for the slippers, he pulled them away, stating emphatically, "No." I tried to start with his sweater and shirt, which he just pulled closer to his body, and he wedged himself deeper in the chair. Stepping back for a moment, I noticed he looked kind of lost; was it humiliating for him to have to have his daughter dress him? My chest swelled with sadness. Though I was trying to replicate the routine mom had for him, he was all off. I knew the Depends needed changing and of course I couldn't just leave him in the chair to sleep, but he wasn't budging. Trying all the techniques of redirecting: "Hey, how about these blue pajamas then?" or "Let's go see if Mom left toothpaste in the bathroom?"—he would have none of it.

I looked around his room as though hoping to find a magic wand I could wave and make it all go away—make the dementia go away, make the frustrations go away, make the heartache of seeing him like this all disappear. I could find no such wand. I did notice, however, the picture he had above his bed of the church he grew up in as a boy, and it hit me. "Dad," I said, "I almost forgot, we haven't said our bedtime prayers!"

Dad prayed on his knees every day of his life until he could no longer get on his knees. Raised Catholic, Dad was dedicated to the tenets of his faith and to prayer. Luckily, the mention of prayer got his attention, so as I attempted again to remove his slippers, I began reciting the Lord's Prayer, then the Hail Mary, then the Lord's Prayer, then the Hail Mary, then both over and over again until he was completely changed, in his pajamas, and safely lying in bed. He had used every word of the prayers perfectly. By the end *I* was huffing and puffing, but he looked peaceful. I made a sign of the cross (he did too) and he let out a big sigh. He was quiet; prayer had brought him back to a place where he "remembered" comfort and God's presence.

As memory disease progresses, it becomes harder and harder for families to do things that have been meaningful together and this is very much true of going to church and maintaining a spiritual life. For families who have been active in church communities, this is a great loss. Families begin missing old friends and miss being in a place that was spiritually comforting. For many people, church was a second home, a second family, and perhaps for decades, families engaged in Sunday worship together, attended church suppers and fairs, served on committees, taught Sunday school, or served on the altar as a Eucharistic minister.

But at some point all that changes as Alzheimer's and dementia progresses. For a while it is well worth the effort to get loved ones to church when they (and you) are still able. It can be very fulfilling for everyone and most church communities are now very understanding about the disease. I recently had a colleague tell me that one of his choir members had stopped singing because his wife's dementia had progressed so far the choir member needed to sit with his wife during the entire service or she couldn't come. The congregation would hear none of it and members took turns sitting with her so the man could continue to sing.

The very last time I took my dad into a church, I knew it was definitely a high-risk situation, so I chose a small local chapel and a less crowded Tuesday noontime service to attend. Given issues around incontinence, fall risks, and other behavioral surprises, I wasn't sure how it would go. As it turned out, this would be one of his "good days." Dad bowed his head at appropriate times, recited most of the responses, and appropriately stood in line for communion. To watch him "remember" all the gestures and words made it a very meaningful outing for us both. Not long afterwards though, it became too difficult (and dangerous) to do even this.

So first, as a family member of someone with dementia, know that if it *has* become too difficult to take your family member to church, that is ok. Don't feel bad about it, don't feel guilty for finding it too much work, and don't beat yourself up over not going. Negative feelings of guilt and failure won't serve you well and will only sap you of your energy. Do, however, grieve the loss of going to church together. This has been a big part of your life and it is sad you can no longer do it. Dementia, as we know, is a series of many small losses over the course of a very long time; losing this part of your life together will take some grieving.

So grieve, and then discover what you still have and what you *can* do.

What you *can* do is still have an active spiritual life together. What you *can* do is invite God into this part of your life. What you *can* do is create new ways of worshipping, praying, and singing together. Whether you are caring for your loved one at home or if they are in a facility, the following ideas are ways to keep God at the center of your very difficult journey with Alzheimer's and dementia. Trying these will help your loved one experience God still in their lives, and this may not be bad for you either. Having God by your side will be so important. On the days when you sit at the kitchen table and cry into your hands, I encourage you to look up and across the table, as God weeps with you and hears your cry.

Here are some ideas and ways to recreate your family's spiritual life in this new phase of living with Alzheimer's or dementia. I also encourage you to read the other chapters in this book, even the one for clergy. You will have the opportunity to do similar work and will have similar experiences as clergy will have in creating meaningful spiritual moments. Your experiences will be different because this is someone you love in a different way, someone you may have shared your life with, but what works for clergy might be helpful for you too.

- First, ask your clergyperson to visit your loved one, even asking him or her to come up with a regular visitation schedule. Gather any family members around when the clergyperson is there and share the visit together. Sometimes the appearance of clergy (wearing a stole or their collar, or carrying a Bible) helps create recognition for what is taking place. Ask them to provide Holy Communion if your loved one is able to receive.

- Have your church office make sure they are mailing your loved one the Sunday bulletins and monthly newsletters, even if they will only look at it and cannot read anymore. Perhaps you can read parts to them; the familiar words and phrases will be of comfort.

- Continue to say grace at meals, especially if they are still joining you at the table. Once we asked Dad to say grace when he was very far into his dementia and he said some amazing and appropriate things.

- Watch church services together on TV. Can you come up with a "ritual" that you do before the service starts like lighting a candle or sitting in certain seats? If they would have gotten dressed up for church, before watching the service, try putting a tie on them or some jewelry if that is what they would have done.

- As you need to remove things from their living spaces for safety reasons, try to find items that can stay and be visible, like pictures of their church, a candle, cross, statues, pictures, rosary beads, and so on. If some of these items are special or family keepsakes, buy "religious" items that you don't have to worry about being broken or disappearing. (Dementia patients are notorious for moving things around and hiding things.) My dad had had that small poster-size picture of the church from his boyhood above his dressing chair for decades. We tried to keep this up on the walls during several of his moves.

- Most importantly, pray together.

Praying with Those Who Have Dementia

Praying in your household might have been something you did together or may have been something members did privately, on their own. If you are more used to private prayer, this may feel different and require some getting used to, but this prayer time can be very special. Family members and caregivers of dementia patients rarely have a quiet moment, so this prayer time has the potential to offer at least a moment of calm in otherwise often stormy days.

If there is a particular time of day that you prayed as a family, continue to do that, and if not, it is never too late to start a new tradition. The following outline can be adapted for use in homes or if visiting family members in facilities. Take what feels comfortable or useful and then adapt it to your situation.

To start, create a "sacred space." Put together a bag or basket of things you can use like a cross, Bible, candle, picture (of Jesus, Mary, St. Francis, or another favorite religious image), special prayer book, set of rosary beads, some colorful linen, or favorite religious object. With all the modern technology we have today, download some favorite hymns on your phone, iPad, or computer. If these aren't tools you have, a small, easy-to-carry CD player works, too.

When visiting them in a nursing home or doing this at home, slowly "set the table" while they watch you (or ask them to help if they can). Don't feel like you have to talk while doing this. I often don't use any words at all. Remember that words aren't what they used to be for people with Alzheimer's and dementia. I realized early on in my work that for this population, holding a cross, running their hands along a picture of Jesus, holding their old prayer book—these things bring back more emotional memory than me babbling on.

Perhaps to start you can play a favorite hymn (for example: "Amazing Grace," "Rock of Ages," "Joyful, Joyful," "Blessed Assurance"). Feel free to sing out loud; you'll be surprised to find that your loved one may start singing with you. (Don't worry if you aren't of great musical talent—they won't tell anyone!) Use the sign of the cross as a signal to begin, or use words like, "Let us pray." Bowing your head and putting your hands together will be a visual cue to prompt them.

You might want to create a special prayer book that they can follow along with. In the chapter on creating a worship service, I have explained the booklet I use in a memory care unit; this might be helpful for you, too. I put together such a book for my dad. It was in a three-ring binder and had prayers with pictures. For the Lord's Prayer I not only had the words of the prayer but a big picture of hands in prayer. For the Prayer of St. Francis I had a colorful picture of the saint surrounded by birds. After a few tries you will find what works for your loved one, what triggers a response, and where they find it easy to connect. Try different music, different prayers, different pictures and prompts until you find the ones that work. Even children's religious books with big colorful pictures can help create connections.

When your prayer time is over, repack your things, slowly and carefully returning them to your bag or basket, folding the linen, putting out candles, and so on. This signals that the prayer time is over.

As with everything we do in caring for loved ones with Alzheimer's or dementia, remember that what works today may not work tomorrow, but might work again next week. It is unpredictable. But keep trying and don't be discouraged on the days when nothing seems to work.

At some point, your loved one will begin his or her journey back to God, and having learned to pray together in this new reality can be of comfort. Sometimes, for people with Alzheimer's and dementia, death comes suddenly with a heart attack, stroke, or other major event. Other times death comes slowly as they stop eating and drinking, stop engaging, and slowly fade away. Sometimes family members will tell me that as death nears, they feel anger toward God for all that their loved one has gone through. They feel angry that they were robed of "growing old with the woman I loved" or they have to wonder, "What kind of a God allows Alzheimer's?" Anger, I assure them, is a completely acceptable feeling, and what's more important is that God wants to know about it. God wants to hear about the anger and the pain and the questioning. Letting God know you are angry is ok. Sometimes we think we should only talk to God when we are saying, "I love you, God," "Thank you, God," "You are wonderful, God"—but that's not true. It's ok to say, "God, I am so angry with you right now." God wants all of who we are, our anger and our praise; our disbelief and our believing; our pain and our joy. It is only in the honest sharing of emotions with God that God can find a way in to heal and comfort.

However death comes, you and your loved one will have experienced God's presence in praying, singing, and worshiping together. Hopefully, you will be able to trust that they will know as they are dying, that God is very present and will remove all pain and hold them gently. The knowledge of God's presence will be a gift to you, too, as you learn to trust that you have done the best you could.

Trust in the midst of this difficult disease can be so hard to come by. I leave you with this quote from Corrie ten Boom, the

Dutch Christian who is credited with having saved hundreds of Jews during the Nazi Holocaust of World War II. She once wrote, "When a train goes through a tunnel and it gets dark, you don't throw away the ticket and jump off. You sit still and trust the engineer."[8] When the time comes, I pray that you, too, will be able to trust the engineer.

8. http://www.brainyquote.com/quotes/quotes/c/corrietenb393675.html

Interlude

Role Reversal

They say that parenting and child roles switch as people grow older.

In one role I am the child, five years old, and my father is dropping me off at kindergarten. I am crying and the teacher has to peel my arms off from around his neck and I watch him walk away. In the next role, I am the grown child dropping *him* off at the nursing home where he will live out his last days, and this time it is I who will walk away.

I volunteered to tell him. We sat alone in his living room. "The doctor said . . . ." (We blamed everything we didn't want him to think was our doing on the hypothetical "doctor.") Today was the day I would tell him he was going to a nursing home. His dementia had progressed to the point he needed twenty-four-hour care, and after ten years of doing that herself, Mom needed a break. So I said it: "The doctor said it isn't safe for you to stay home anymore; you need to be somewhere where there are more people around to make sure you are safe. Mom doesn't feel well and is getting tired."

He started shaking his head slowly, with a firm determined look on his face. He clasped his hands together and put them in front of him, looking straight ahead. This was always a sign that he was "thinking." I continued, "So we have to try this, at least until we know you are safe." There I go, cushioning it by saying maybe he'd come back home even though I knew there would be no turning

49

back. I am only human and couldn't bring myself to tell him this was it. Hope springs eternal, wasn't there always hope? Wasn't there a *chance* he could get stronger and come home? The rock in my stomach knew otherwise.

After a long silence he spoke. "Nope." Amazing how clear and on target someone with dementia can suddenly be.

"Trust me Dad, it isn't what we want but we don't have a choice. The doctor says you aren't safe at home." I knew my voice was losing its confidence.

"Who is the doctor, call him!" Dad said. Damn that clarity! Instantly all the doubts and second thoughts raced back: I should have pushed harder to keep him home; he isn't *that* bad yet; the recent episodes of trying to escape at night, the hallucinating that there were people in the apartment, the swinging at Mom, the incontinence—those were all just freak things that would never happen again, right? Damn.

"Dad, you always took such good care of our family; you took good care of Mom. This is another way that you can do that," I said. He just stared ahead, hands clasped in defiance. Someone once told me to remind the person with dementia of what they were good at and appeal to who they were—like a mom who took care of babies and a dad who was head of household—so I tried to appeal to the provider he always was, but it wasn't going to work this time.

I knew Mom was waiting at the nursing home. That was the plan, I would tell him, she would take care of all the paperwork, and we would meet there around noon. The advice we had been given was not to give Dad days to think about it, so we talked about it the night before and after a demonstration of "no, not going to do that, never," an episode of *Little House on the Prairie* distracted him. He forgot about the conversation. He was loveable, cooperative, and went to bed without problems.

That was last night. This was today.

"Well," I finally declared, "not much more to talk about. I'll get your coat. You need the bathroom first?" I got up, remembering how important it is to demonstrate what you wanted done. I put on my sweater. Since he always needed the bathroom, this felt like a good way to at least get him out of the chair and upright; from there maybe he would forget what we were doing and why. He watched me walking in circles like a nut and just shook his head no.

"All right, let's watch some news then." Distract and redirect, distract and redirect. That had been the mantra for years. I figured I would sit for a while, then try it all over again. I gave him a cold drink, we watched the news, and twenty minutes later I announced it was time to get our jackets. He wouldn't even look at me. It was time to call in the reserves.

When my husband arrived we agreed going for lunch would be a way of at least getting him out the door, especially if it was to his favorite place in the harbor where he liked to watch the boats. "How about I get you a burger and a martini?" my husband asked. It all felt so foolish, lying to him, tricking him, but the alternative was calling the EMTs and removing him by force. While this felt dishonest, at least it had some level of dignity compared to being forced into an ambulance gurney. We had a nice lunch, he had a martini. I had thoughts of kidnapping him and bringing him to my house and telling everyone else in the family I had changed all the plans. Instead, I drove to the nursing home where the staff and my mom were waiting out front.

"What in the hell is this?" he said looking out the car window. I got out and opened his door.

"Sorry, Dad," I said, "I have no choice." This was it. It was done, I was the betrayer and had delivered as promised. It felt awful. He at least got out and walked over to where my mother was and sat with her on a bench. The staff gathered around them and began friendly hellos and nice to meet yous. He smiled at all the attention and was the gentleman he had been all his life.

I stepped back from the scene. The nurses and my mom motioned to me that they would take it from there, they had a plan. I walked back to the car and watched, and at that moment it was the first day of kindergarten all over again. At that moment I was five years old watching him leave. I was five years old wanting to run and hold on to him so nothing scary or bad would ever happen. I was five years old again, needing my dad, but this time, leaving *him* behind.

CHAPTER FIVE

Tools for Ministry

——•◆•——

Do not cast me off in the time of old age;
   do not forsake me when my strength is spent.
(Psalm 71:9)

W hat will I say? What should I do? She won't know who I am. What can I talk about? Will any of this make a difference?

As clergy, ministers, chaplains, or lay spiritual leaders, you would not be alone if, when visiting people with Alzheimer's or dementia, you found yourself asking these questions. Despite your desire to make God part of their day, you may feel frustrated about how to do it and anxious about your visit. This ministry is different than we are used to, and most of us have not received special training to care for those with dementia. We have had pastoral care and counseling courses and done clinical work, but seminaries aren't far behind the culture we live in which does not like to talk about aging. Pastoral training in seminary probably covered issues such as death and dying, mental health, divorce, grief and loss, and cancer, but probably not conversations about Alzheimer's and dementia.

The good news is that things are beginning to change and many seminaries are beginning to integrate conversations about ministry with the aging into pastoral care classes and training. Asbury Theological Seminary in Kentucky now offers a special master's degree program in Aging and Spirituality[9]; and in April of 2015, Columbia Theological Seminary launched a new certificate program through its Center for Life Long Learning[10] for older adult ministries. Spiritual caregivers can begin to explore this ministry, but even these programs miss a big piece of the picture. Most conversations about Alzheimer's and dementia, like the programs mentioned above, are centered on older adults, but as we know, not everyone with dementia is elderly. So ministering with those who have dementia can be anxiety provoking, and some days it may feel easier to balance the church budget than to visit Mrs. Jones in the nursing home who has Alzheimer's.

Despite our anxieties, however, as people of faith we already have what we need to do this work because God is already there. God is already by Mrs. Jones's side waiting, loving, holding, and being. Since God is already there, all we have to do is journey with them to help them make that connection. Our outreach to those living in care facilities is so important since most nursing homes and senior living facilities do not have spiritual care staff or

---

9. http://asburyseminary.edu/academics/degrees/master-of-arts/m-a-in-aging-and-spirituality/

10. www.ctsnet.edu/older-adult-ministry-certificate-program

spiritual services for their residents. Hopefully that will change in the future, but funding chaplaincies and spiritual care positions is not on the top of Medicare's agenda.

So if we don't embrace this ministry, who will? People with Alzheimer's and dementia already feel so isolated, alone, and shut off from the world (as do their families). Our job is to help them make connections that can draw them out of places of silence and loneliness to where they can remember that God has not left them alone. I know this work can be a little scary, but remember, the phrase "be not afraid" is used more often in the Bible than almost any other phrase . . . so be not afraid, God will go with you.

Tools for Clergy, Chaplains, and Pastoral Caregivers

> Then I heard the voice of the Lord saying, "Whom shall I send, and who will go for us?" And I said, "Here am I; send me!" (Isaiah 6:8)

As you are sent, here are suggestions or "tools" for ministry with Alzheimer's and dementia.

Rule number one is: *just show up*.

Just show up, and know that you don't have to have all the answers; you don't have to know exactly what to do. The most important thing you bring is the willingness to show up and be in the midst of what can feel unpredictable. Some visits may be a little uncomfortable with patients who are verbally inappropriate, agitated, and fidgety, or even hard to sit with because of soiled clothing, runny noses, or bad smells. Other visits will be tender and gentle with a person who just wants to hold your hand or rest her head on your shoulder, or who makes you laugh because of the carefree simplicity of their spirit.

In the years I worked as a hospice chaplain, I consistently experienced anxiety before visiting a patient with dementia. It's not that I am an anxious person, it's just that the job of making spiritual connections felt so important. I knew in my heart of hearts that a connection with God could make all the difference. But how to do that changed with every visit, so anxiety was real. This was especially true when visiting those with dementia because I never knew *how* I was going to find the person or *what* odd situation I might suddenly find myself in (and odd situations can occur pretty regularly with this population). Visits with dementia patients are so different than visiting the sixty-year-old with cancer or the eighty-year old with heart disease. The "tools" we were taught in pastoral counseling classes don't always apply to people with Alzheimer's or other dementia diseases. I will admit to often feeling completely unequipped when I began working with this population on a regular basis. What do I do? How can I help? But the more I visited them, the more I came to discover that these unknowns are actually the beauty of spiritual care. *We* don't have to know, *we* are not in charge, and *we* don't decide what will happen. God already knows, God is already there, so we don't have to have the answers, just the willingness to try.

So the first thing we can do is get out of our own way. While every pastoral visit should allow the person we are visiting to direct the care given, this is especially true of dementia patients. Follow their lead, watch for where they are, and just be present. Teepa Snow tells a very good story about a pastor who rushed in too quickly with his own agenda.

Pastor James had come to see a parishioner living at a facility where Teepa advises. Teepa watched as the pastor came into the patient's room, Bible in hand, walked over to her bedside and said, "Miss Mary, this is Pastor James . . . what would you like to pray for today?" Teepa then watched Pastor James's horror as Miss Mary grabbed both his hands and lunged them into her abdomen saying, "You've got to pray for a bowel movement, please tell the doctors to get it out!" Miss Mary was clearly in physical pain and could not think about praying for another thing until they prayed for a bowel movement, which they did, with Teepa's help. Praying for bowel movements might be a little departure from how we are used to ministering, but nevertheless honors where people are and what pain is real to them.

Approaching the visit with a heart that is a "clean slate" will allow you to observe, adjust, trust, and then respond as the Spirit works. So rule number one is *just show up*. God will take care of the rest.

The second rule is: *be easy with yourself.*

Pastoral care is at the heart of why most of us get into ministry. There is nothing more rewarding than a good pastoral visit in which the one suffering physically, mentally, or spiritually is suddenly renewed by our presence. If you've ever offered absolution to the guilt ridden, you know what I mean. If you've ever prayed for healing over someone in pain and they "felt better," you know what I mean. If you've sat with someone dying and been able to talk about the nearness of God, you know what I mean.

Visits with those who have dementia, however, usually won't come with affirmations of our ministry, and that can make us wonder if we are helping at all. Deep conversations aren't going to happen and most aren't going to tell us what we love to hear, that we have made a difference. I have to constantly remind myself not to let my ego get in the way of ministry with the memory impaired, or any ministry for that matter, but especially with this population. Letting go of an expectation of gratification allows me to stay out of my way and trust that even if my visit seemed "useless"—Mary never opened her eyes when I prayed; Bob walked back and forth in his room while I tried to sing; Kim just got frustrated, yelling to help her escape—I may never really know the impact of my being there.

Sometimes though, if we pay attention when visiting, we may find simple cues that we have helped that person reconnect with God. One Ash Wednesday, I gave ashes to a man sitting in a wheelchair in our memory care unit, making the gentle sign of the cross on his pale thin skin. When he looked up at me, his eyes were filled with tears. Something had hit home, maybe the familiar words, maybe the way it felt on his forehead. I'll never know, but he got it. Another example is a time after prayers and songs in my small group, a woman left humming "How Great Thou Art" and then began repeatedly saying, "beautiful, beautiful, beautiful." I can't tell you how many crosses I have lost to patients who didn't seem to be making a spiritual connection but suddenly were so calmed by the sight of a cross they held onto it with the strength of a superhero. (So I let them keep it, of course.) The point is, watch for cues; they won't be the ones we are used to like, "Thank you, Pastor, that was a lovely visit," but they will be there. Even if the visit feels like an absolute disaster and (it seems) nothing has worked, as anyone who cares for people with dementia will tell you, what works today might be different tomorrow, and by next week it will all be different again. So be easy on yourself; there is no such thing as a meaningless visit.

A third skill in this ministry is: *show, don't tell*.

The biggest lesson I've learned in providing spiritual care to those with dementia is the use of visual and auditory prompts to fill spaces words no longer can. Pastoral visits to those with dementia should involve as few words as possible, which can be tricky for those of us used to doing a lot of talking.

To start with, one of the best words you can give up as you begin this work is the word "remember." It is amazing how often I find myself using it and what a silly thing for me to say. I think about how many times I said it to my own dad in his years in dementia: "Dad, you remember the place we used to go in Vermont, right, you remember, the place with the big gazebo by the lake; you remember, we used to cook outside and play cards all night, right, Dad, you remember?" Well, no, he doesn't remember.

We all do it—ask them to remember. It's like asking a three-year-old to do physics or someone with a broken leg to go for a run; they can't do it, they don't have the tools anymore to recall and remember. Sometimes it seems *we* have forgotten that they have memory loss, and so no, Dad doesn't remember the gazebo by the lake, and asking him six times isn't going to make him. He might eventually shake his head "yes" after I've asked him feverishly nodding *my* own head up and down for so long, but he is probably just copying me when he eventually nods his. It may have made me feel better, but asking him to remember didn't help him do so.

The same is true of visiting people from our congregations. We do well to give up the "remember" questions: "Remember how we decorated the church with wreaths during Advent?" or "Remember Mary, the one who sings in the choir; you remember Mary, Mary says she is praying for you." Well, no, they probably don't remember Mary, so rather than "telling" them, "show" them.

Rather than *asking* if they remember decorating the church with wreaths, is there a picture of the church you can bring to *show* them? With today's technology, can you show a video on your iPad of the decorating being done? Better yet, bring in a fresh wreath, let them hold it, help run their fingers over it, invite them to smell it—that fragrant pine smell can bring back emotional memories of special times.

Rather than *asking* if they remember Mary from the choir, can you bring in a CD with music from the church's choir? This kind of prompt will help them "remember" on an emotional and spiritual level, which is very real. While Mary the singer might be a very nice person, it is unlikely the person with dementia will recollect who she is; but to hear Mary singing "Amazing Grace" on a CD (even better yet, bring Mary in to sing), this has the opportunity for the patient's emotional memory to bring them right back to their pew . . . third one from the front on the left.

Music will be one of the most powerful tools of this ministry because for all people, music has connections to personal memories. Music will offer you a way to "show" your ministry in a way that spoken words can't. Think of songs from your past and the memories they stir. I cannot hear the 1985 Dire Straits song "Money for Nothing" (also known as "I want my MTV") without remembering a summer on Martha's Vineyard when I was a college student, waitressing to save money for a semester abroad in Europe. Whenever I hear, *"We've to move these refrigerators, we got to move these color TVs,"* I am nineteen again, suntanned, and carefree. Music has the power to take us places, places that have emotions, and it is the emotional memory of Alzheimer's patients we want to reach.

Someone recently asked me whether this was a good idea, after all some music reminds us of sad things, like a hymn sung at a loved one's funeral. This person asked, "Wouldn't playing music that makes them sad not be good?" Indeed we want to protect and comfort people, but sadness is part of being human and sad emotions are real. The person with dementia is still human; to be a complete human means to sometimes feel sad. Should a song we play trigger a sad memory and cause someone to cry, we have perhaps offered them a release of pain they otherwise had no outlet to release. And so we sit with them through the tears. Even if they can't explain what they are sad about, we can offer, "I can see this song has a lot of emotions for you," or just a hand to hold, or a tissue, or a shoulder to rest on. By doing so we validate who they are and what they feel.

Teepa Snow uses music in her work and tells the story of the power of spiritual music. She was once at the bedside of an Alzheimer's patient who was dying. The patient's family was feeling helpless over what to do in this moment of great loss. Teepa suggested they sing one of her favorite church hymns, "You Are the Potter." As the family sang, the patient opened her eyes, sat up, and said, "You are all here." The family had found a way to be with her through music. They thought she was gone, but through a favorite hymn were able to find a way to be together in her final moments.

A fourth tool for this ministry: *pack a bag!*

Throughout this book I have given examples of visual "prompts" that help people with Alzheimer's and dementia reconnect with their faith. As clergy visiting parishioners with dementia in nursing homes or in their own homes, having your own bag that travels with these items can enhance your visit and help you to feel confident.

A communion kit is always a good and familiar tool. I keep battery-operated candles in mine, a linen, colorful crosses, sometimes even things like a sprig of holly during Advent, colorful plastic eggs in Easter season, paper butterflies in spring, snowflakes in the winter. The sight of a chalice and paten is a great visual cue, as are the little wafers. (I had a person once take the wafer and write her name on it and put it in her pocket. Oh well, things happen!) If administering communion to someone with dementia, check first with family or staff that they are not a choke risk since swallowing problems become prevalent as the disease progresses. In your bag bring a Bible (consider using older versions of scripture translations that might be more familiar to them), your church's worship book, photos of your church, prayer beads, music, or statues. I once had a children's book of Bible stories with colorful pictures and a panel down the side that you could touch to play a song that corresponded to the Bible story. It was a great tool that I had to leave behind somewhere and never saw again. (Note: Often people with dementia can find it hard to "give back" an item that has been given to them, so you might want to consider what you bring, in the event you have to leave it behind. Family and facility staff can be notified if indeed you have been unable to retrieve a special item.)

You might also be able to videotape one of your Sunday services to have on a CD or iPad that you can watch with your parishioner. Remind whoever makes this video to show faces of people worshipping, singing and praying, and close-up shots of things like the consecration of the Eucharist and children taking Holy Communion.

There are lots of other good tools to use on visits that might just be fun and enhance your time together. There is an organization called Nasco that supplies all sorts of items for those who work in education fields and with seniors. Their website[11] has a

---

11. www.enasco.com

special section for Alzheimer's patients where you can find things like picture books for conversation starters, interactive books, picture card sets, small games, puzzles, stuffed animals, and sensory trays. On the Alzheimer's Association website, in the caregiver section, there are also ideas for things to do with patients. Chapter six offers a sample "service" you might be able to adapt for use with those whom you visit.

One more tool: *your congregation.*

As a final tool in ministry with people who have Alzheimer's and dementia, consider how to create a dementia-friendly congregation if there are members attending who have the disease. Take a look around your church to see if there are ways of making your facility safer so families feel welcome. Some ideas include:

- Placing pictures as signs around the church that cue things like where the bathrooms are located or that stairs are ahead.
- Most facilities are equipped now to handle wheelchairs and the needs of those with mobility issues, but making sure halls and bathrooms are well lit and that there are handrails in the bathrooms will help those still ambulatory but a little shaky on their feet. Look for other items around the church that could be fall risks like area rugs that are not secured.
- Invite the person with dementia to sit in on a Sunday school class or worship service where the program is simpler. They also might enjoy attending a choir practice and listening to the music.
- Encourage the congregation to wear nametags at all events to help the person with dementia remember names. (At my parent's fiftieth wedding anniversary party, which was just

three weeks before my dad died, we asked everyone who came in to put a nametag on to help him remember. While these were people in some cases he had known for fifty years, the nametags helped him retain some dignity.)

- If someone is still physically capable, is there a way they can be of use around the church, stuffing envelopes for example, putting out napkins at the coffee hour, or sweeping the church hall?

- Ask friends of the person with dementia if they can keep an eye on him or her while that person's spouse or family member talks to friends, has coffee, or spends some time getting spiritual support with you.

Interlude

Spiritual Care for All

While this book focuses on care given to the person with dementia, a whole other book could be written about caring for their families. Most family members will tell you that living with dementia can bring an unimaginable flow of emotions ranging from anger, frustration, and sadness to moments of joy, tenderness, and special time together. Family members are generally exhausted (mentally and physically) from caregiving, confused about what decisions to make, feeling very isolated, grieving the life they dreamed of, and often guilt ridden because they wish it would all just go away.

While we might be tempted to suggest to a caregiver that they stay active with their church as it would be "good for them," their reality is that it is hard to make a Wednesday Bible study when they've been up since three o'clock in the morning with a spouse trying to escape from the house. It is hard to get to church on Sunday when they are embarrassed at how they look, unable to get to the hairdresser in months because they can't leave him alone and can't afford paid help. As good for them as *we* imagine it would be for them to continue singing in the choir, we have to remember their reality. Singing Christmas carols might not feel like it used to as they mourn the loss of a life they dreamed and face an uncertain future. We often want to encourage them to go to support groups, which are great for a great many people, but not for everyone. For some it is just one more thing they can't balance or squeeze into an already complicated schedule. My mother always said that her inability to make a support group made her feel like she had failed at yet another piece of caregiving.

So these families need some special care. Some won't want a lot of people coming and going; some will worry their loved one would not want others seeing them in such a condition. Others might welcome company. In the end, I think what most families want is just someone to listen. Yes, there are practical things church communities can do to help, like meals, offering to run errands, even provide some "sitters," but I find most just want to tell you their story. They want someone to know how sad they are, how tired, how overwhelmed, and usually too, how privileged they feel to care for their family member. It is good to give families a place to talk about loss, grief, and the way dementia steals a person from you— little, by little, by little.

Families can benefit from having someone to talk to about things like care directives ("When Mom stops eating, should we do a feeding tube?"), or how to tell Dad he can't drive anymore. (By the way, doctors will write a "prescription" that says "Do Not Drive," and families can put this on the refrigerator which helps the person with dementia not blame the family for taking the keys away.) Families can benefit from someone to talk to about end-of-life wishes, when to sign a DNR (do not resuscitate), when to stop tests and treatments, and when to call hospice. These are hard conversations to have, especially because, as clergy, our opinions carry some weight for those we pastor. Helping families uncover their own thoughts and feelings about these matters is a gift to them, as is supporting their decisions, even if they differ from our point of view. Being willing to walk this long road with them is sometimes the best and only thing we can do to make it any easier.

As clergy we can also benefit from knowing the local resources when families begin this journey. Are there members of the congregation who work in health care, social services, mental health, or geriatric care specialties that might help you put together a list of resources? Having conversations with family members to find out their needs and let them know you are eager to have them as part of worship services might ease their anxiety. Church-wide education programs about dementia with guest speakers from the community can also help create a community that is compassionate about the struggles of families living with the disease.

When someone has received a diagnosis of Alzheimer's or dementia, it can feel for that person, and for their families, that they are suddenly drowning in an angry ocean where the waves are just crashing around them, and when they reach out their hand for somebody to keep them from going under, often all they get is another medical form to fill out, a toll-free number to call, or another book someone says they should read. I'd like to think we, as spiritual caregivers, are the hand they find when they reach through those crashing waves, and our response is not a form or a phone number, but rather the assurance that while we may not have all the answers, we are willing to go with them.

To be spiritual care providers for the future, God calls us to respond and tend to these important members of the flock, a flock that in the coming years is only going to grow. While this ministry may look and feel different from what we are used to, giving people the dignity of worshiping together, praying together, and singing together in the midst of memory loss, honors the face of God in each person.

The Bible tells us a few things about those who are aging. Psalms 92:14a (KJV) reminds us "they shall still bring forth fruit in old age." As spiritual care providers, this population has so much to teach us and their teaching is the fruit they bring forth. Being with them in worship, prayer, and song makes us part of a movement toward more holistic care of those with dementia, one that remembers the Spirit. By helping them reconnect with their faith and spiritual practices, we are letting them know that God hasn't given up on them, and most importantly, that they haven't been forgotten.

CHAPTER SIX

Worshiping with the Memory Impaired

One thing I asked of the LORD,
   that will I seek after:
to live in the house of the LORD
   all the days of my life,
to behold the beauty of the LORD,
   and to inquire in his temple.

For he will hide me in his shelter
   in the day of trouble;
he will conceal me under the cover of his tent;
   he will set me high on a rock. (Psalm 27:4–5)

As spiritual care partners we can help create the comfort of being in God's house for those who suffer from memory loss. Whether a nursing home, memory care unit, living room, or a church hall, God's home is where God's people gather. For those with Alzheimer's and dementia, opportunities to sing hymns and say prayers will be a reminder of the safety, protection, and companionship that is God's house, with a God who remembers them and has indeed created a "safe dwelling place."

Below is a sample of the service I have used in several memory care units and nursing homes over the past years. It is my dream that one day every nursing home and memory unit will have at least a once-a-week worship service for its residents, if not daily. It amazes me how many facilities have bus trips for lunches by the ocean, Frank Sinatra sing-alongs, and arts and crafts, but very few programs that address issues of spirituality. In fact, my afternoon worship service in a memory care unit was recently co-opted by a bus trip. The facility got a van they could use the same day and time as my program, so rather than twenty residents I now often have just four or five. While I agree the residents need outings, worship services offer care of the spirit in a way that a trip to the muffin factory can't.

Teepa Snow from Positive Approach says that religious worship is critical to overall care for those with dementia diseases because it allows them to express and experience feelings. "The 'spirit' part of a person is always there," she says. "Although there are so many losses on the outside, it doesn't lessen who they are inside." Just because someone's speech or physical abilities aren't functioning, Teepa says that inside there is still a flame in each person and worshiping together allows them to "be" who they are.[12]

Worship can take many forms: traditional prayers, songs, meditation, chanting, a slide show of religious images, even visits by

---

12. Teepa Snow, interview with author, May 8, 2015.

little animals. The goal is to help people reconnect. Family members, friends, clergy, chaplains, and nursing home staff can do this. I believe the worship service I have developed works because it is designed to bring out what they *can* still do and *how* they can still worship. It is simple but rich. Over the years I have tried things that didn't work (like going around the circle to say what we would like to pray for, or reading long passages of scripture) and so what has worked I have incorporated into a program I call "Songs and Prayers."

For my program, the prayers and hymns I choose are ones that are traditional and most familiar to the larger Christian population. In my experience, they are among those most easily remembered. This service lasts about half an hour, which usually feels like just the right amount of time.

My service is just a sample of what you might use. There may be songs and prayers that are more familiar with your population or your loved one, so be creative. For clergy connected to a congregation, consider offering such a service on a weekday in your church hall. Reach out to local Alzheimer support groups and let them know you are offering it for those members who might not be coming on Sunday mornings because it is just too difficult.

What follows is the service I developed, described so you feel as though you are in it. I will explain why I do certain things. At the end are some notes that might help.

Welcome to my service of Songs and Prayers.

To Begin

When residents arrive for Songs and Prayers, church is ready just like it would be on Sunday morning. The altar is set, candles are lit, worship booklets are on chairs, and calm music is playing.

The altar is a short, round coffee table in the center of a circle where there are chairs and spaces left open for wheelchairs. The candles are of the battery-operated type (for safety), but flicker nicely and look real. There is a colorful wood painting of Jesus on the altar, as is a cross, a set of rosary beads, some paper butterflies, and a Bible. Since research on Alzheimer's patients shows that because of vision changes they are most likely to notice bright colors, the altar linen is a bright, multi-colored tablecloth from Mexico.

When residents arrive I help them find a chair. To some I hand a "worship booklet" (see note 1 below). Some residents will follow along with the words, some will just look at the accompanying pictures in the booklet, others will play with the pages, and others won't want (or be able to hold) a booklet at all.

When I begin, I stand to get their attention, holding my hands open as a clergyperson would in any church service. I thank them for coming and invite them to make the "sign of the cross" to begin prayers. I also say "The Lord be with you" for those who come from traditions where the sign of the cross is less traditional. Both the sign of the cross and the "Lord be with you" phrase serve as cues that we are about to begin. In making the sign of the cross myself, I use big, slow gestures so it is clear what I am doing, and I use the traditional words of "Father, Son, and Holy Spirit." While many traditions are replacing those words with gender-neutral ones like "Creator, Redeemer, Sanctifier," traditional words have the best likelihood of triggering a response.

I have my computer with me for the songs we are going to use. I have a little portable speaker so that the music is loud enough, remembering that this population usually has hearing loss too. The songs I use are versions that have fewer verses and in some cases are slower. I use hymns alternating with the prayers, and integrate a few moments of "show and tell" type actions.

It flows like this:

Song: Our first song together is "Amazing Grace," using the three verses that are most popular. The verses are printed in large type on a bright yellow sheet in the worship booklet.

Prayer: After singing, our first prayer is Psalm 23. To introduce this, I take out a puppet of Jesus (this is just a very simple handmade puppet one of my girls made at church camp years ago). Holding my puppet, I say he is someone special who goes by many names: Lord, Messiah, Friend, Rabbi, Christ, Jesus, Son of God . . . and that one of my favorite names for him is the Good Shepherd.

Early on in my work, I used to ask if they knew who the puppet was. I have since learned that this can be frustrating and sometimes embarrassing for them as they try to word-search a name. The goal in caring for this population should always be preservation of their dignity, so I have learned to just say the name myself, avoiding embarrassing moments when they have to say, "I don't remember." Depending on who is there that day, I might add a few words about the Good Shepherd, like he is the one who helps when we feel alone and helps show us the way when we feel lost. I then begin the prayer and they join in.

Song: Since I have the Jesus puppet out, I will often mention that the children in my church like to sing a special song about him, and then I simply start singing *"Jesus loves me this I know . . ."* and again, they join right in.

Prayer: The next prayer is The Lord's Prayer. To introduce this, I walk around the circle showing them one of my props: for example, the colorful painting of Jesus surrounded by children where Jesus is holding up bread and wine. I might offer a few words about Jesus as a teacher and how he taught his friends to pray. The picture of the bread and wine helps to recall Eucharist in church. I let them touch the picture and hold it. I also have a real chalice and paten on the altar and so I quietly pick them up, holding them up as one would in church, adding the words, "Remember me." I then say, "Let us now pray in the words that Jesus taught us to pray . . . *Our Father, who art in heaven . . . ."*

Song: The song to follow The Lord's Prayer is "How Great Thou Art." I transition into the song by saying something like: "When we think of God, do we think God is little or is God big? Is God small or is God great?" I use hand gestures for tiny and big, and usually offer the answer for them, the hand gesture being the prompt for the word big or great.

Prayer: The next prayer is the prayer attributed to St. Francis. This is a good one to use, not only because they recognize it, but also because it gives us a chance to talk about animals. St. Francis, of course, is known as the patron saint of animals and the natural world. I will often ask who likes dogs; who likes cats; who likes snakes? (Often I accompany the words with sounds like barking or meowing. I have sometimes brought pictures of my pets to show them. Quite often they will break into stories about their own pets from when they were little. Talking about how much we love pets makes for an easy transition into the prayer, *"Lord, make me an instrument of your peace, where there is hatred let me sow love . . . ."*

After the St. Francis prayer, I use "Hail Mary." For those who grew up Roman Catholic, especially for women, praying to Mary was of great comfort. Mary is revered as the intercessor, the one carrying prayer requests to heaven. (In the facilities where I work in Eastern Massachusetts, there are large populations of Catholics, so this is a good prayer to use. However, if working in a place that has a more mainline Protestant population, this prayer may or may not be as helpful.) To introduce the prayer, I pick up the rosary beads from the table and hold them in my hand. I hold up three fingers, letting them know we will pray it three times.

> *Song:* After these two prayers, I transition to the next song, "Here I am Lord," by saying that Mary and Francis said "Yes" when God asked for their help. I remind them that they can be God's helpers too. Some of this conversation is too wordy and more than some residents can process, but for some I believe it is a reminder that they are still useful and valuable to God.

After the song, I bring out my friend Giggles. This is my favorite part of our time together. Giggles helps us offer our prayers.

Giggles deserves his own explanation, so you will hear more about him soon.

> *Song:* To end, I use the song "This Little Light of Mine." First I point to the candle on the altar and say a word or two about "God's light," often leading them through one verse of "This Little Light of Mine." But when that is done, I have a very jazzy, New Orleans-style version of the "This Little Light" that I end with because it is very upbeat. We clap, snap, and hold our hands in the prayer position when we sing "Amen." It is uplifting and a perfect ending.

When the service is done, I stand and offer a blessing using big arm motions of "Father, Son, and Holy Spirit" and then come around taking each person's hand, saying "God's peace be with you." They know, they understand the gesture, and very often return God's peace. It is a beautiful moment.

To Conclude

When all is done, I put on some quiet music again and let them watch as I "unset" the altar, repacking my things. I don't use a lot of words, but slowly take each item, put it in the bag, fold up the linens, and make sure Giggles waves good-bye before going in the bag.

Some of the most coherent things I have heard these residents say is often after our time of prayers and hymns. Yes, there are sometimes tears too, as their hearts remember emotions, even when words can't explain them. Some tears I know are of sadness, but some I know are happy tears too. Tears are ok. I truly believe that by walking them through the words, sounds, and gestures of "church," they connect with the powerful feelings that worshiping evokes for all people of faith. It truly lifts up what we know to be true, that wherever two or three are gathered in God's name, God is there. God hasn't forgotten them.

Interlude

Giggles

Giggles is something I discovered by chance nearly a decade ago, and his story deserves telling so that you can appreciate its effects on those with Alzheimer's and dementia.

Years ago I was one of three families going to New Hampshire for a long ski weekend. One of the families was bringing their children, including a ten-year-old whose birthday it would be while we were there. The other couple was bringing their mother, who was in her early seventies and had Alzheimer's. For the child's birthday I bought what I thought was a great gift, a little stuffed toy monkey who, when you flick on his switch, rolls around the floor laughing.

Well, ten-year-olds have more interest in electronics than giggling monkeys, but our friend's mother with Alzheimer's fell in love with it! She laughed and laughed and laughed when I put the monkey on the floor. Time and time again, and hour after hour, it held her captive in joy and laughter as the monkey rolled around. The monkey's laugh is completely contagious and this woman could not contain her own laughter. The entire weekend, while others skied, she and I sat on the couch and watched the monkey roll around, and did we laugh.

Well, I've purchased a few more monkeys since then, and the one that attends our worship service in the memory care unit is called "Giggles, the Praying Monkey."

When I bring him out from my travel bag, I introduce him saying: "When we say our prayers and sing, we feel so close to God, our hearts feel so happy and we are filled with joy." I hold my hand over my heart to make the point as I continue: "When we feel so close to God, this is what happens." I switch Giggles "on" and place him on the floor in our circle. Faces light up, laughter begins, and people are transformed. Even the grumpiest of residents are drawn out of their shell by Giggles. I try my best to make the connection between prayer, song, God, and joy, but I tell you, Giggles does it better than anyone.

When time with Giggles is over, I offer a blessing, whatever feels right to say at the moment. I bow my head, hold my hand up offering a physical sign: Father, Son, and Spirit. Most certainly heads and eyes are lowered; residents often bless themselves with the sign of the cross.

Giggles brings the joy of God in the midst of our worship circle, when words may no longer suffice.

CHAPTER SEVEN

From Where Will My Help Come?

———◆•◆———

I lift up my eyes to the hills—
   from where will my help come?
My help comes from the LORD,
   who made heaven and earth. . . .

The LORD will keep you from all evil;
   he will keep your life.
The LORD will keep
   your going out and your coming in
   from this time on and forevermore.
                    (Psalm 121:1–2, 7–8)

Where will my help come from?

How to care for someone with dementia, where to find the right kind of help, and how to advocate for patients and families will be some of the hardest things people face while living with Alzheimer's and dementia.

Families will have to wrestle with questions like how to keep a loved one safe, when is the best time to take away a driver's license, when should they stop leaving them alone, where should they live, who will care for them? On top of all of these emotional questions will be the myriad of obstacles to address like sifting through health forms, insurance policies, long-term care programs; setting up a health care proxy and power of attorney in order to legally sign for the person with dementia; looking at Medicare and Medicaid coverage, veterans' benefits, hospice service, prepaid funerals, and other daunting financial challenges. While most people will be trying to just make it through the day, there will be bank forms to fill out, long phone conversations with insurance companies, and an overload of information to sift through.

If you are a family member, you already know this. If you are clergy, families will tell you about this; they will cry about it, feel sad and overwhelmed about it, and yet still have to find a way through. While helping people deal with issues of care for their loved one might not immediately sound like a spiritual or pastoral issue, it is hard to tend to the spirit when the body is exhausted and the mind overwhelmed. As spiritual caregivers, this chapter will touch ever so briefly on some of the supports and challenges those you minister with will face.

There is good news and bad news about the logistics of caring for people with dementia. The good news is that there are many people and numerous organizations that now exist to offer various types of help; there are many online resources and a growing number of community resources to support people and families. The bad news is that while some of these resources are free or covered by insurance, many are private pay, making it difficult for some to afford the support they need, and deserve.

To start, here are some ways families can find help.

Many people will choose to hire a **geriatric care manager** (GCM). GCMs are professionals who are trained in the care of older adults and have had education in fields such as social work, psychology, nursing, health care, or gerontology. They work as advocates for those who hire them, helping to navigate the health care system and come up with best possible care plans. They are generally connected in the industry and know where to find nursing homes, private help, adult day care programs, and other elder services in communities. They do all the groundwork so that families can make more informed decisions. They are paid privately by the consumer and are worth the costs for those families who can afford it. There are numerous websites with lists of GCMs, and they can also be found through organizations like AARP, the Alzheimer's Association, and the National Association of Geriatric Care Managers.

Because of the complexity of financing a loved one's care, many find that hiring an **elder law attorney** to assist in financial planning not only alleviates stress but can save money in the long run. Topics they help with include things like trusts, estate planning, coordination of health benefits, guardianship issues, and Medicaid questions. The National Academy of Elder Law

Attorneys[13] provides links to these specialists throughout the country.

Most communities now also have **adult day care** programs that provide well-needed coverage and care of people with dementia during traditional work hours, Monday through Friday. Programs vary; some are covered by veteran's benefits, and most provide transportation to and from the program. Along with providing caregivers time to work or do other tasks, the programs offer time for socialization that is so important. Living with Alzheimer's or dementia can be so isolating; attending a program offers time to interact with other people and be entertained. My dad never wanted to stop working in his law practice, so when we had him in a day care program we dug out his old briefcase and put some files and folders in it for him. It helped get him on the van some mornings because "his clients were waiting for him."

As clergy with some knowledge of these services, we can help families learn how to advocate for care. Depending on the circumstances, we can accompany them on doctor visits, to the emergency room if something happens, or to get results after a test. Especially if a caregiver does not have family around to go with them, having another person present can be helpful since so often at doctor appointments, someone who is overwhelmed will walk out only having heard half of what the doctor said. By accompanying them we can help ask questions and make sure they understand what is said.

I said earlier that there was good news and bad news around the logistics of caring for someone with dementia. The good news is all the support and services mentioned above. The bad news is that

---

13. www.naela.org

many of them, being privately paid, are not accessible to average and lower income families. Without these professionals to help make decisions, many families end up with fewer choices, with care directed by Medicaid or insurance polices, and in facilities that are outdated, overcrowded, and with staff underpaid and undertrained to work with dementia patients.

Especially if a family is trying to keep a loved one home, the costs of doing so can add up quickly when outside help becomes necessary. As hard as we tried to keep my father home, it became too expensive for us. Though he had been prudent in saving and spending all his life and had planned for the future, his savings weren't enough and my siblings and I weren't in a financial situation where we could finance his care. Dementia can be a very long disease requiring years and years of help. For a while we had the assistance of paid home health aides whose fees ranged from $15.00 to $30.00 an hour. Aides often work for private companies or visiting nurse associations, but even for a few hours here and there, this quickly began to eat away at savings. Even a few hours a day became too expensive, and when he began being up at night and wandering, we needed even more coverage because his safety was at risk. In the end he became a Medicaid patient in a nursing home that did their best to care for him.

As people of faith, the discrepancy in care for the wealthy versus lower income populations should be a concern and as well as an ethical, moral, and spiritual issue. If only the wealthy can afford good care if they develop Alzheimer's or dementia; if only the wealthy can afford to keep their loved ones at home; if only the wealthy can go to facilities that are clean and warm with employees specially trained in dementia care—where is the equality of care?

As people of faith trying to live into our Baptismal Covenant to "respect the dignity of every human being," shouldn't we be advocates for good quality care that includes *all* people with Alzheimer's and dementia, regardless of wealth and status?

We also have to ask hard questions about income and wages when we consider the reality for CNAs (**certified nursing assistants**) who take care of our loved ones at two o'clock in the morning, cleaning soiled sheets and pacing halls with the restless ones. These caring men and women don't make enough to feed their families or have a livable income. Across the board, hard-working CNAs are severely underpaid. According to the U.S. Labor Department's Bureau of Labor Statistics,[14] the national average hourly wage for a CNA is $12.62, but can vary depending on what part of the country you are in, going as low as just over $9.00 an hour in some places.

Much I hope will change in coming years. Better options, better facilities, better support, and better care for the millions of people with dementia must be talked about. While the search for cures and treatments is ongoing and millions of dollars are being spent on research (which is so needed), people are suffering from the disease right now. Millions are sitting alone in nursing homes, millions of families are crumbling under the weight of caregiving, millions are spending every last dollar they have, and millions of others just feel lost and abandoned. While we wait for a cure, and while we wait for the industry to improve, we in the spiritual community are in the midst of it: We are in the trenches with the people—in the congregations and nursing homes, and with families impacted by the disease, which means we have the opportunity, if

---

14. www.bls.gov/oes/current/naics3_623000.htm (accessed July 17, 2015).

not the responsibility, to create better lives for them now and advocate on their behalf.

The psalmist asked, from where will my help come? It is the
same cry that anyone who has ever faced dementia care has asked.
Spiritual caregivers who understand even the basics of these challenges will be of great value.

Interlude

Navigating the Journey

Mary has Alzheimer's and has a habit of walking out the front door at all hours of the day and night. Her daughter cannot coax her back inside and they argue heatedly. Harry's dad can't remember his own son's name or the year he taught him how to play baseball. This hurts Harry emotionally every time they see one another. Chloe yells at her husband every time he visits her at the care facility that he never comes to visit, when he's already been there four times in the past week. He blames himself and takes each verbal assault personally.

Each of these incidences could be relieved if the family member had access to information about living with someone who has dementia. I often wonder how families and care partners of those with dementia survive if they haven't had access to such information or special training. I have heard family members say they don't visit his or her loved one with Alzheimer's very much anymore because it is just too hard, just too sad.

I understand that. It is hard, and sad.

Which is why I encourage people to do some learning and even, if they can, get training on living with dementia, and if they can afford it, to get professional help to navigate the journey. There are many, many books on the topic, probably too many to ever imagine reading, but it is worth the bit of knowledge from what others have learned. Many communities are now offering informational pro-grams at places like senior centers, and there is even online training like Teepa Snow's Positive Approach. (See Resources on page 109.)

By the time my dad was diagnosed with dementia and the symp-toms began progressing, I was so grateful that because of my work, I had received dementia care training. Not that information and training made it any less painful and sad to watch him decline, but at least I had some tools.

For example, I knew that as someone with dementia he would have little short-term memory (like who visited yesterday) but often his long-term memory would be quite intact. He had spent his life as a lawyer, so when his house was sold I saved a few boxes of his very old files. In them were articles he had saved about his career, being elected as a city councillor in town, and stories of people that had been part of his life.

Since it's often hard to find things to do with people with dementia, sometimes when I would take him to my house for an afternoon, I would pull out one of these folders and even suggest he had some work to finish on them. Sometimes he would spend upwards of an hour looking through them.

There was one afternoon I particularly remember. The folder I had given him had some of his handwritten campaign speeches, a list of campaign helpers, newspaper articles, and election results around his run for city councillor in the 1970s. He was quiet, occupied, and engaged in stacking and restacking the papers, often using his finger to follow along on a page he appeared to be reading.

After an hour with the file, he said he was "done working" and closed the folder. "Time for . . . for . . . for . . . ." He lifted his hand to his mouth several times mimicking drinking something, searching and searching for a word. I said, "Time for a beer!" He smiled, nodding his head and rubbing his hands together with excitement like a little child just offered an ice cream sundae.

While I searched for a glass, he came over to me with a stack of papers from the file. He said he was done with them and wanted to throw them out. (Without some training my emotions would have found me arguing with him about not throwing them out, that *I* might want to keep them, doesn't he know that I've lost so much of him these old papers are often the only thing that links me to who he was? But I knew arguing doesn't work, nor would me being overly emotional help anything.) I pointed the way to the trash can (knowing I could pull them out when he wasn't looking), but he said no, not there, and went to the fireplace (which was not lit thankfully) and put them inside of it on top of the ashes from last night.

All the training and information in the world can't prepare you for moments that are just so sad. As I watched him put the papers in the fireplace, I watched his face grow serious and pensive. I thought I saw a note of "giving up" in his eyes. Did he want to burn the past? Was he letting go? Or giving up? Did he not want to remember that person in the pictures on the newspaper article and campaign flyers? Was that person dead, no sense saving the pictures anymore?

We sat at the kitchen table; he drank his glass of beer and ate a bowl of Goldfish, which he began tossing to our Boston terrier named Henry who loved to catch them in his mouth. This was one of their favorite games. The heaviness in Dad's eyes left and he was back to being silly, which is why he got along so well with Henry.

After dinner, I drove him back to the nursing home where he cheerfully greeted the staff. Sometimes these drop-offs are disasters, and sometimes easy—welcome to dementia, the land of unpredictability.

When I returned home, I went to the fireplace and took out his papers. I brushed the soot off of the pictures of him as a young man, speaking at some podium, other papers with his scribbled handwriting on them, others with lists he had made. I knew I would want to have them later when he was gone. They are a part of a story I only know bits and pieces of, and for now I wasn't ready to let go of the pieces I did have. As children we don't really know who our parents are when we are growing up, and often dementia will silence the opportunity to find out. Sometimes we realize all the questions we have when it is too late to ask them. So I stacked his papers and stories neatly, just as he would have done, and returned them to the box where I was saving them. Dementia is such a thief.

CHAPTER EIGHT

A Good Death

After my awaking he will raise me up;
and in my body I shall see God.
I myself shall see, and my eyes behold him
who is my friend and not a stranger.

Happy from now on
are those who die in the Lord!
So it is, says the Spirit,
for they rest from their labors.[15]

W e all want the people we love to have a good death—comfortable, peaceful, pain free, surrounded by those who love them.

---

15. From the Burial of the Dead, Rite Two, The Book of Common Prayer, (New York: Church Publishing Incorporated, 1979), 491, 492.

My dad didn't have the death I wanted for him. At the end, it seemed to me, he suffered physically and emotionally. He had a sudden change in mental status (perhaps another TIA?) that resulted in increased agitation, which required hospitalization and an increase in medications. When he returned to the nursing home it was too late to think about bringing him home to my house with us to die; he was already dying. The hospitalization had been too much. We took up camp by his bedside at the nursing home, taking turns talking, holding, praying, listening to music, and counting the seconds in between breaths. This we did for five grueling days, until he died.

There were two things that most surprised me in the moments after his last breath. The first is that oddly enough, my very first thought as I hugged him good-bye was that I hoped he was ok with the choices we had made for him. Throughout his years living with dementia, as a family we had to make some tough choices: deciding he should close his law practice; deciding he shouldn't drive; deciding he shouldn't be left alone; deciding he wasn't safe to live at home anymore; deciding not to perform life-sustaining measures. The funny thing about making those decisions is that they came with such a both/and set of emotions. It felt horrible to have to make them, and yet such an honor to be part of his care. To leave him behind in a nursing home will always be one of the worst days of my life, and yet, wouldn't he have wanted us to make the best decision for him and our family? Helping decide "comfort measures only" started a course of action that was irreversible and ultimately allowed him to die, and yet, isn't allowing the body to do what it naturally needs to do when it is old and sick, isn't that not only an act of compassion, but what he would have wanted?

All these things rushed through my head in the seconds after his death. I even spoke it out loud, "Daddy, I hope you are ok with our choices." I said it, leaning over his body after the nurse nodded her head, confirming that breath was his last. What a crazy thing to say, I later thought. At the moment of death, I didn't say, "I love you" or "good-bye" or "thank you" (though I had said these things many, many times before). Why was the need for some kind of absolution the first thing my heart uttered?

In retrospect it is probably because as care partners of those living with dementia, things are not black or white, and for all of us, feelings of second-guessing, regret, or even guilt may be very real. In time I've been able to live into what I always say in my pastoral role to those making such decisions: that the decisions we make, when they are made out of love, are always the right decisions and the best "next" right thing—always harder to practice what we preach. But still, at the end, there is no one to hand us a checklist that says we did all the right things. People who die from other diseases often have the opportunity on death's bed to let their loved ones know how grateful and pleased they are for the care they have been given; this isn't true with dementia deaths. With his last breath, the decisions were over, and so yes, my strange uttering of, "Daddy, I hope you are ok with our choices."

The second thing that surprised me when he died was actually the absence of relief. I had always thought that after such a long road, after such a long decline, after so much trauma and loss and suffering, after all this I expected to feel relief that his struggle was over, and yet I didn't. People sometimes say death due to dementia is like death by a million small cuts; some say to die from the disease is like a series of multiple deaths over and over and over. I have heard others say they felt like they lost their loved one not once at death, but several times long before a last breath was drawn. All of those things are true, and yet I felt no relief when he died and that remains a mystery to me. Perhaps it is because I still miss him, or perhaps it is because, while I would never want him back as he was when he died, suffering physically and I believe emotionally, I still wish we had more time together. I spent more time with him in the last three years of his life than I did the previous thirty. Perhaps we all feel that way—that just one more year would have been nice.

As spiritual caregivers, when death arrives for the families we are ministering to, there will be all kinds of emotions and feelings. Death from this disease comes in so many forms. Some will go through a long process of withdrawing deeper and deeper until they are finally bedbound, unable to eat, drink, or communicate; they eventually become weaker and weaker and slowly and quietly fade away. Some people living with Alzheimer's and dementia die more quickly from a physical event like pneumonia, heart attack, or major stroke. Often a fall leads to a broken bone or other injury that begins a process of decline. Sometimes there is a change in mental status requiring them to be sedated, which can also begin a process of decline. Since we usually have to rely on body language and nonverbal cues to understand how someone with dementia is feeling, without the words it is sometimes hard to understand what they need, what hurts, and what might help. And sometimes, in the end, we just don't know for sure what was the final cause of death.

The end of life can be complicated. If families haven't had conversations about death prior to a turn in someone's condition, when death appears near, they are sure to feel overwhelmed by decisions.

Studies have shown that people with advanced dementia are much more likely to receive "heroic" measures than people without the disease because of family members afraid to make end-of-life decisions. It is *always* hard to decide *not* to begin an IV line or put in feeding tubes. A family once said to me, as they declined feeding tubes, that they felt like they were starving their mother to death. I had to remind them it wasn't *they* who were preventing her from eating, but the disease and a tired body that was ready to go. Too often families begin tube feeding, intubation, or other life-sustaining measures because it feels awful not to, and then they have to make the difficult decision to remove them. It is our instinct to try to make people feel better and get better. Choosing to let them go feels counter to everything else we have done. I can't tell you how many times I have seen people try to force someone to eat, only to have the person push away the food, not open their mouth, or become extremely agitated. All our lives we cook and feed people, it feels against human nature to *not* feed someone; all our lives we spend trying to chase away death—to allow it to arrive can feel like giving up.

As spiritual care providers, there is much we can do to educate families about the progression of the disease and the body's natural process of shutting down when it is sick. Our bodies are meant to die, yet across the board we over test, over treat, and over-extend measures to keep people alive. It is hard to let the body do what it does naturally. It is hard to decide for another person that there is no longer any quality of life. At these moments, families benefit from a compassionate spiritual advisor that can help them deal with their guilt and confusion, and help them plan for the best possible death, including the use of hospice care. Hospice care sooner, rather than later, can often mean a more peaceful death, without hospitalizations, invasive treatments, and options of staying home.

What this all means, as I think about it and pray about it, is that there is much more we can be doing to help people with dementia die in dignity and with comfort. By having spiritual care as part of their lives throughout the earlier years with dementia, when death is near, we—and they—are able to draw comfort from our faith.

When I recently had a conversation with my friend Joan about how worried I was that my dad's death wasn't a "good death," she reminded me of a hospice nurse we both knew who used to say that almost everyone wishes they could rewrite the circumstances of their loved one's death. "But we don't get to," said my friend. Pausing, she very wisely reflected, "I'm going to guess that's how God felt too. I bet God wishes he could have rewritten how his Son died." Which is how I end this book. With faith . . . knowing that faith does not make dementia go away, but certainly carries us through the journey; and faith makes us certain, certain that God is with us through it all and especially when the very last breath is drawn. Amen.

What Happens at the Time of Death
By The Reverend Colette Bachand-Wood

"What will it be like when I die?"

First, God will come and hold your two feet in God's hands; He will rub them gently and remember all the miles you walked, all the miles through both hard times and joyful times; and He will help you remember only the JOY . . .

Next, He will hold your legs in His hands and give thanks for their strength that carried you on earth . . .

Then, She will take your upper body and place Her hand on your chest. Because of this you will feel warmth in your heart; because of this, your heart rate will slow since She will be holding its anxiety . . .

Then, God will gather your arms in His and remember all of the heavy loads you carried . . . arms that carried so much and have grown weary, and God will free them of their burden . . .

Then, God will touch your ears, removing anything bad they ever heard. She will caress them with words of love, gratitude and thanksgiving; they will be warmed by God's gentle whisper that "You are my Beloved" . . .

Then God will gather your face in Her hands, look deeply into your eyes and watch you as your breathing slows; as your breathing slows God's breathing will take over; as yours ends God's continues, increasing, accelerating, beating strong and melodious until your breath has become One with His . . .

And then it will become clear,
all the pain will end,
all questions will be answered,
great arms will lift you,
you will understand
there will be no more waiting . . .

And all will be a great AMEN.

Interlude

Saying Goodbye: Two Poems

"When Christ shall come with shout of acclamation
And lead me home, what joy shall fill my heart."[16]

In the End: Waiting

Waiting,
didn't know how vacant it would feel
to wait for death.
A slate of non-emotion
wishing for everything and nothing;
counting numbers of breaths
and spaces in between.
Intervals of 10/30;
ten seconds of breath and thirty of none,
ten and thirty, ten and thirty, ten and thirty.
In the thirty, there is nothing,
no air, no sound, no movement.
What happens in between?
What do I do when the thirty seconds of nothing,
turns to 60 seconds then to 90
until no breath at all?
Are you still in there?
Or did you leave quite some time ago?

---

16. "How Great Thou Art," *Lift Every Voice and Sing II—Pew edition*, (New York: Church Publishing Incorporated, 1993), hymn 60.

What is this space of non-space, of non-being,
of non-sense, *but complete sense,* of dying?
What am I waiting for?
Is it you that isn't letting go . . .
. . . or is it me?

Two Weeks Later: Can't Find You Anymore.
I can't find you anymore,
I can't find the places, or the smells or the things
I can't feel your presence, or feel you close by
It is a deep gone-ness I never imagined.
Vacancy.
While I don't believe it is forever,
the moment now is dark and gone.

I can't find you anymore
in the family gatherings,
everyone is gone home,
stories have stopped,
memories tucked away,
cards stacked on the piano,
flowers all faded and brown.

I can't find you anymore
in the coffee and muffins
or the smells from the bathroom
or your humming or whistling
or your frustrated talk, words, and meanings
aching to be released but trapped.

I can't find you anymore
in the Sunday afternoon meals
or ball games or news reports,
grilled cheese, chocolate cake at my house.
Afternoon drives
where you read every sign.

I can't find you anymore.
Snatched away,
vanished
medicated, and
then only the breathing
until it was no more.
And now,
I just can't find you anymore.

Putting Together a Worship Service

-------◆-◆◆-------

The Worship Booklet

Depending on where people are in their disease, they may or may not be able to use a worship booklet. I always offer one since holding a prayer book was very much a part of worship life for most people and it seems natural to have something in our hands. Here are some ways to set up the booklet:

- Use sturdy one-inch three-ring binders of varying colors (colors, colors, colors are key in working with Alzheimer's patients); the hardcover binder is easy for them to hold and the bright colors help them to see.
- When printing a prayer or song, use large type fonts and try to find an accompanying picture to go on the page since those who can't read might have memory recall from the

picture. For example, the page I use for Psalm 23 has a comforting picture of Jesus holding a sheep and carrying a staff, the page with the Hail Mary has a large set of rosary beads, and the page with the St. Francis's prayer has a picture of him surrounded by colorful birds.

- Using different color pages in the booklet will make it easier to find the page by color. For example, in my book the page with the Lord's Prayer is blue so I can prompt people by saying, "Turn to the blue page."
- If there is access to a laminating machine, laminate the pages to make them sturdy and easier for their hands to hold. If not lamenting, plastic sheet sleeves work too. (The plastic covering also makes them easy to clean if you are in a health care facility and need to comply with regulations concerning cleaning.)

An alternative to a worship booklet is to have the words of the prayers and songs, along with picture cues, on a whiteboard or flipchart for all to see.

Enlisting an Assistant

If the facility has an activity person on duty during your service, I usually ask them to help those holding a booklet to find the right page. Family members visiting can also assist with this.

Your Appearance

Alzheimer's research shows that patients respond more to caregivers wearing colorful clothes. Simple bright red or blue shirts and sweaters are good. Bright lipstick on women also helps them focus on smiles.

Tone of Voice

It is always tempting to "talk down" to Alzheimer's patients in a voice one might use with a small child. I have found that a voice tone that is calm, slow, and not high pitched elicits the best response and respects their dignity.

Administration of Holy Communion

While I often feel compelled to offer communion to those at the prayer service, given the high incidents of choking among this population, I have opted not to offer a service involving the Holy Eucharist.

Prayer Objects

Often people have busy hands, looking for things to clutch, hold, or play with. I have several things I give these folks including small wooden crosses and squishy balls that have words like "hope," "love," and "peace" on them. I even have small colorful beach balls that say "Jesus Loves You." Sometimes playing with these things relaxes them and they are able to participate and listen along.

Disruptions

Last but not least, expect disruptions. This is not Sunday service where the congregation can follow expectations. During these services, people may wander from seats, drop worship books, say strange things, yell at their neighbor, have issues with incontinence, or just outright leave. Resident safety is always the first priority, so get staff assistance if the disruptions are dangerous. Otherwise, go with the flow, always try to redirect someone who might be agitated, stay calm, and absolutely do not take anything personally.

The Prayers

The Lord's Prayer

Our Father, who art in heaven,
Hallowed be thy Name.
Thy Kingdom come.
Thy will be done on earth,
As it is in heaven.
Give us this day our daily bread.
And forgive us our trespasses,
As we forgive them that trespass against us.
And lead us not into temptation,
But deliver us from evil.
For thine is the Kingdom and the power
and the glory
Now and forever,
Amen.

Psalm 23 (KJV)

The Lord is my shepherd;
   I shall not want.

He maketh me to lie down in green pastures;
   he leadeth me beside the still waters.

He restoreth my soul:
   he leadeth me in the paths of righteousness for his name's sake.

Yea, though I walk through the valley of the shadow of death,
   I will fear no evil;
      for thou art with me;
      thy rod and thy staff they comfort me.

Thou preparest a table before me in the presence of mine enemies:
   thou anointest my head with oil;
   my cup runneth over.

Surely goodness and mercy shall follow me all the days
         of my life,
   and I will dwell in the house of the Lord for ever.

Hail Mary

Hail Mary, Full of Grace
The Lord is with thee,
Blessed art thou amongst women
And blessed is the fruit of thy womb, Jesus.

Holy Mary, Mother of God,
Pray for us sinners,
Now and at the hour of our death.
Amen.

The Prayer of St. Francis

Lord make me an instrument of your peace,
Where there is hatred, let me sow love.
Where there is injury, pardon.
Where there is doubt, faith.
Where there is despair, hope.
Where there is darkness, light.
And where there is sadness, joy.

O divine master grant that I may not so much seek
To be consoled as to console,
To be understood as to understand,
To be loved as to love;
For it is in giving that we receive;
It is in pardoning that we are pardoned;
And it's in dying that we are born to eternal life.
Amen.

Appendix C

Resources

————◆•◆•◆————

Websites

Aging Life Care Association (ALCA)—Formerly the National Association of Professional Geriatric Care Managers, this non-profit association offers expertise and promotes the interests of those who provide care for the aging. There are regional chapters throughout the United States.

www.aginglifecare.org

Alzheimer's Association—All kinds of information, chat rooms, tips, research, and contacts to local support groups. Every state has a local chapter. Clergy can browse through AA's library of articles written about spirituality and dementia.

www.alz.org

American Society on Aging—An organization that supports the commitment and enhances the knowledge and skills of those

who seek to improve the quality of life of older adults and their families.
www.asaging.org

Clergy Against Alzheimer's—An organization that represents a wide spectrum of faith traditions and includes experts in pastoral care for those with Alzheimer's, elder care issues, hospice care, dementia friendly programs and communities, and Alzheimer's education––all with a focus on the broader subject of spirituality and aging.
www.usagainstalzheimers.org/networks/clergy

The Forgetting: A Portrait of Alzheimer's—Short and excellent films about Alzheimer's disease offered by PBS, including "Is It Alzheimer's?" and "What Is Alzheimer's?," that explain this disease.
www.pbs.org/theforgetting/watch/pocket.html

The Genius of Marian—A moving story and video of one family's experiences with Alzheimer's.
http://geniusofmarian.com

Health Care Interactive—An extension of the Alzheimer's Association, a program called "essentiALZ" provides online training for caregivers of all types.
www.hcinteractive.com/CompleteCatalog

Memory and Music—This is the organization that provides resources and training for their program that uses iPods to enhance the lives of those living with dementia.
www.musicandmemory.org

Positive Approach—Teepa Snow travels throughout the country, and her training programs are offered regularly for professionals and family members.
www.teepasnow.com

Print

Brackey, Jolene. *Creating Moments of Joy for the Person with Alzheimer's or Dementia: A Journal for Caregivers*, 4th edition. West Lafayette, IN: Purdue University Press, 2008.

Carey, Louise. *The Hedge People: How I Kept My Sanity and Sense of Humor as an Alzheimer's Caregiver.* Kansas City: Beacon Hill Press, 2009. A daily devotional for caregivers with touching and humorous stories, as well as daily prayers and reflections for spiritual growth.

Genova, Lisa. *Still Alice.* New York: Gallery Books, 2009. The story of one family's experience with early onset Alzheimer's which has been made into a movie.

Morse, Louise. *Worshipping with Dementia: Mediations, Scriptures, and Prayers for Sufferers and Carers.* Oxford: Monarch Books, 2010.

Otwell, Pat. *Guide to Ministering to Alzheimer's Patients and Their Families.* Philadelphia: Taylor & Francis, 2008.

Stokes, Graham. *And Still the Music Plays: Stories of People with Dementia*, 2nd edition. London: Hawker Publications Ltd, 2010.